Cambridge Elements 

Elements in Ancient Philosophy

edited by
James Warren
University of Cambridge

ARISTOTELIAN ONTOLOGICAL PRIORITY AND METAPHYSICAL GROUNDING

Bryan C. Reece
Baylor University

CAMBRIDGE
UNIVERSITY PRESS

Shaftesbury Road, Cambridge CB2 8EA, United Kingdom

One Liberty Plaza, 20th Floor, New York, NY 10006, USA

477 Williamstown Road, Port Melbourne, VIC 3207, Australia

314–321, 3rd Floor, Plot 3, Splendor Forum, Jasola District Centre,
New Delhi – 110025, India

Cambridge University Press is part of Cambridge University Press & Assessment,
a department of the University of Cambridge.

We share the University's mission to contribute to society through the pursuit of
education, learning and research at the highest international levels of excellence.

www.cambridge.org
Information on this title: www.cambridge.org/9781009547963

DOI: 10.1017/9781009433617

First published 2026

A catalogue record for this publication is available from the British Library

*A Cataloging-in-Publication data record for this Element is available from the Library
of Congress*

ISBN 978-1-009-54796-3 Hardback
ISBN 978-1-009-43365-5 Paperback
ISSN 2631-4118 (online)
ISSN 2631-410X (print)

Aristotelian Ontological Priority and Metaphysical Grounding

Elements in Ancient Philosophy

DOI: 10.1017/9781009433617
First published online: March 2026

Bryan C. Reece
Baylor University

Author for correspondence: Bryan C. Reece, bryan_reece@baylor.edu

Abstract: Many think that reality is structured such that some beings are more fundamental than others and characterize this structure in terms of 'grounding.' Grounding is typically regarded as explanatory and as exhibiting certain order-theoretic properties: asymmetry, irreflexivity, and transitivity. Aristotle's notion of ontological priority, which inspired discussions of grounding, also has these features. This Element clarifies Aristotle's discussions of ontological priority, explores how it relates to other kinds of priority, and identifies important connections to metaphysical grounding. Aristotle provides numerous examples that appear to impugn ontological priority's order-theoretic coherence. This is Aristotle's "Priority Problem." But Aristotle has an independently motivated solution that eliminates the threat from each of the apparently problematic examples and explains why such examples are ubiquitous. The Element argues that a ground-theoretic analog of Aristotle's solution to the Priority Problem addresses recent challenges to grounding.

Keywords: Aristotle, grounding, priority, fundamentality, metaphysical explanation

ISBNs: 9781009547963 (HB), 9781009433655 (PB), 9781009433617 (OC)
ISSNs: 2631-4118 (online), 2631-410X (print)

Contents

1 Introduction

1.1 Purpose, Scope, and Method

This Element is meant to highlight a way in which careful consideration of Aristotle's views and of a widely discussed topic in current metaphysics can be mutually informative. I will argue for several original claims. Some of these are meant as contributions to scholarship on Aristotle, others to current metaphysics. But my overall argument is that concepts sharpened in recent debate can help us to clarify a problem for Aristotle, the solution to which in turn elucidates what a unified, principled way of resolving an important current dispute would require.

A secondary purpose of this Element is to provide a conceptual, technical, and bibliographic resource for readers who might be more familiar with Aristotle than with current literature on metaphysical grounding and vice versa. I here deal with two very large sets of literature and therefore cannot discuss all of the important contributions to them. An appendix collects various technical descriptions that appear in the main text.

1.2 Grounding and Aristotle

Both in ancient times and more recently, many philosophers have been attracted to the idea that reality is structured in such a way that it has multiple layers or levels, some of which are more fundamental than others. Hydrogen atoms might be reckoned more fundamental than H_2O molecules, and these in turn than the Atlantic Ocean. One might also suppose that a Platonic Form, Large, is more fundamental than particular large things, or that Socrates is more fundamental than the singleton set {Socrates}. Many philosophers have also thought that such a fundamentality structure can be understood in terms of 'grounding,' such that one item is more fundamental than another if and only if the first grounds the second. (We can reuse the examples just given: Hydrogen atoms ground H_2O molecules, which in turn ground the Atlantic Ocean. The largeness of large things is grounded in the Form Large. Socrates grounds his singleton set.) Even cursory inspection of recent literature in metaphysics reveals the enormous current enthusiasm for this idea.

There are, however, various forms of skepticism about the aptness of the grounding idiom for understanding relative fundamentality. These often involve claims that other notions, such as identity and supervenience, obviate grounding because they do the theoretical work that it is supposed to do. This kind of skeptical challenge to grounding has provoked a lot of responses. I want, though, to mention another kind of skepticism. Some years ago it was suggested to me in conversation after a Q&A session that attempts to clarify the structural features of grounding are idle because they have been stipulated by recent authors.[1] (The idea is basically that 'grounding' is an unnatural, gerrymandered predicate with no historical foundation or non-stipulated relationships to useful notions.) I think that this suggestion is mistaken.[2] For one thing, it rests on a misunderstanding of why people have become so interested in rigorously clarifying the notion. Various prominent proponents of the aptness of the grounding idiom are aware that they are regimenting a notion that has a long history. Some connect it immediately to Aristotle, of course. It is also increasingly recognized that Bernard Bolzano (*Wissenschaftslehre* vol. 2, part 3, §§198–222) in 1837 rigorously discussed the nature of ground and consequence (*Grund und Folge*) in ways that anticipate many of the contours of current debates. Bolzano does not seem to have viewed this project as a new one but rather as a clarification of ubiquitous Neoscholastic Aristotelian commitments. He explicitly describes his account of grounding as continuous with Aristotle and the Peripatetic tradition. Bolzano thinks that his *Grund* is what Aristotelians writing in Latin called *ratio* or *principium*. It seems, then, that if we are to conduct a responsible appraisal of the aptness of the grounding idiom for theorizing relative fundamentality, we should do so in light of the history of its deployment. This overall project goes beyond what I can accomplish in this Element and must be postponed for future work, though I will say something later in this section about two of Bolzano's Aristotelian predecessors. I propose here to focus on the relationship between structural features of Aristotle's notion of ontological priority and of grounding as understood in recent literature.

If relative fundamentality is to be understood straightforwardly in terms of grounding, then grounding must share its structural features. I will focus on a widely discussed proper subset of these. Relative fundamentality is clearly asymmetric, irreflexive, and transitive. It is incoherent to suppose that the Form of Humanity is more fundamental than Socrates and that Socrates is more fundamental than the Form of Humanity, that Socrates is more fundamental than himself, and that the Form of Humanity is more fundamental than Socrates and Socrates than a sculpture of Socrates but the Form of Humanity is not more fundamental than a sculpture of Socrates. Grounding's aptness for theorizing relative fundamentality depends in part, then, on whether grounding is also asymmetric, irreflexive, and transitive, that is to say, on whether grounding induces a strict partial order on, for example, facts, truths, propositions,

---

[1] Particularly influential discussions of the notion of grounding are Correia (2005, pp. 60–64; 2010); Fine (2001, 2012); Rosen (2010), Schaffer (2009); and Schnieder (2011).

[2] See also Reece (ms-a).

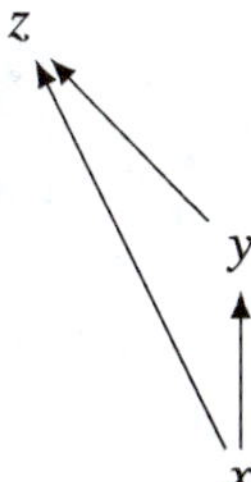

Figure 1 Directed acyclic graph of grounding's order-theoretic properties.

properties, property instances, objects, and so on. Informally, this means that ground and grounded are never convertible, nothing grounds itself, and the grounded's ground's ground must ground the grounded (grounds are inherited). More formally, a strict partial order has the following properties, which I enumerate using two alternative styles of notation that appear in the literature, the first a relational predicate '$\lhd$' (the negation of which is '$\ntriangleleft$') and the second a sentential operator '$<$,' both of which feature grounds to the left (with variable arity) and grounded to the right:[3]

	Predicate	*Sentential operator*
asymmetric	$\forall x, y(x \lhd y \rightarrow y \ntriangleleft x)$	$\dfrac{\phi < \psi \qquad \psi < \phi}{\bot}$
irreflexive	$\forall x(x \ntriangleleft x)$	$\dfrac{\phi < \phi}{\bot}$
transitive	$\forall x, y, z(x \lhd y \wedge y \lhd z \rightarrow x \lhd z)$	$\dfrac{\phi < \psi \qquad \psi < \theta}{\phi < \theta}$

These structural features of grounding can be represented by a directed acyclic graph (Figure 1), where the direction is that of ground to grounded.

---

[3] I adopt '$\lhd$' for the relational predicate from Korbmacher (2018a, 2018b) and '$<$' for the sentential operator from Fine (2012). (Correia, 2005, p. 60 uses the reversed symbol that Korbmacher uses but as a sentential operator rather than as a relational predicate.) It is unimportant for my purposes whether grounding is best expressed by one or the other of these. As is common, for the sake of readability I will write as if grounding is a relation and assume that my points are translatable since I take no stand on what kinds of entities are referenced in grounding claims. (Part of the point of using a sentential operator, as, e.g., Correia, 2005, 2010, Dasgupta, 2017, deRosett, 2023, and Fine, 2001, 2012 prefer, is for the sake of neutrality on this point. Those who weigh in on what kinds of items are referenced in grounding claims include Audi, 2012, p. 686, Bolzano, 1837, part 3, §203, Korbmacher, 2018a, pp. 162–163, 166, Rosen, 2010, p. 120, Schaffer, 2016, p. 75, Schnieder, 2020, p. 100, and Wilhelm, 2020.) Following others on both sides of the debate about whether grounding induces a strict partial order on its domain, I restrict attention to what Fine (2012) calls "strict ground" rather than "weak ground" since the latter is trivially reflexive. I will mark Fine's (2012) distinctions between full/partial ground or immediate/mediate ground only when necessary. Of course, transitivity is limited to mediate and partial ground since full immediate ground is trivially intransitive.

Most who regard grounding as a coherent, unified notion useful for current metaphysics think that it indeed induces a strict partial order on the relevant items (facts, truths, propositions, properties, property instances, objects, etc.).[4] The idea that grounding is asymmetric, irreflexive, and transitive is not new and it has an Aristotelian heritage.[5] It is now recognized with increasing frequency that Bolzano (*Wissenschaftslehre* vol. 2, part 3, §§198–222) offers a rigorous defense of grounding's asymmetry (§202, §§208–209, §211, §219), irreflexivity (§204 and §218), and transitivity (§217).[6] (Again, note that transitivity is limited to mediate and partial ground since full immediate ground is trivially intransitive.) Bolzano does not see his description of grounding in general, or his specification of its order-theoretic properties, as fundamentally new. While he does think that previous deployments of the notion of grounding, largely those by German logicians of the preceding generation, stand in need of regimentation, he sees his ideas about grounding as part of a continuous heritage that runs from Aristotle through, for example, Boethius, Avicenna, Averroes, and Scholastic and Neoscholastic Aristotelians. Among this last group is, whether Bolzano knows it or not, Sebastián Izquierdo (*PS* tom. 2, disp. 15), who argues that priority in nature is transitive (q. 7, prop. 1, para. 68–73), asymmetric (q. 7, prop. 2, para. 74–76), and irreflexive (q. 7, prop. 4, para. 78–80).[7] Centuries before Izquierdo, John Duns Scotus (*PP* cap. 2, §9) argues that an essential order is irreflexive, asymmetric, and transitive.[8]

Why would theorists of today or of the past think that grounding has these order-theoretic properties? One important reason is this: There is broad support for thinking that grounding is explanatory, whether it is, involves, backs, or is accounted for by explanation, and similarly broad support for thinking that in order for grounding to be explanatory it must be asymmetric, irreflexive, and transitive.[9] A good explanation should not simply repeat the explanandum.

---

[4] On the issue of whether grounding is a unified notion, see the prominent challenges by Koslicki (2015) and Wilson (2014), as well as replies by Berker (2018) and Cameron (2014), deRosett (2023), and Nolan (in press). This debate is anticipated in part by Schaffer (2009, pp. 376–377). Koslicki (2020) summarizes such challenges and comments on the way in which doubts about whether grounding induces a strict partial order on its domain contribute to skepticism about grounding.

[5] The earliest use in English of the relevant sense of 'transitive' of which I am aware is by De Morgan (1856, 114) in the course of extending Aristotelian syllogistic.

[6] For an exploration of connections between Bolzano's theory of grounding and Aristotle's theory of priority, see Malink (2020, 2022). For more on Bolzano's theory as such, see Roski (2020), Roski and Schnieder (2022), and Schnieder (2014).

[7] See Embry (2018) for a thorough discussion of Izquierdo's remarks on priority.

[8] See Ward's commentary in John Duns Scotus (2024) for further explanation.

[9] Audi (2012), Bennett (2017), Correia (2005, p. 53), Dasgupta (2017), deRosett (2013, 2023), Fine (2001, 2012), Kovacs (2022), Litland (2013, 2015), Raven (2013), Rosen (2010), Rubenstein (2024), Schaffer (2012, 2016), Schnieder (2011), Siscoe (2022), Skiles and

Neither should it be circular. Furthermore, if x partially explains y and y partially explains z, then we should expect that x partially explains z. All of this requires, of course, holding the type of explanation constant: If x explains y, then y does not explain x in the same way, though it could be explanatory in some other way of x. To use one of Aristotle's examples, walking could explain health as what in part brings it about, but health could explain walking as at least part of one's purpose for doing it.

I want to mention briefly at this point a couple of further features that grounding is typically thought to possess because of its explanatoriness: non-monotonicity and hyperintensionality. I will have more to say about these later (pp. 46, 52). Very roughly, grounding is non-monotonic if and only if the set of grounds of something grounded, just as the set of explanantia of an explanandum, cannot be arbitrarily expanded. For example, suppose that the constitution of Athens both at least partially grounds and is somehow involved in explaining Athens being a democracy. It would be unsafe to infer that the constitution of Athens and the number of hairs in Solon's beard ground and are somehow involved in explaining Athens being a democracy. By 'hyperintensional' I mean that the substitution of necessarily coextensive, even co-referring terms in a grounding claim can change its truth value. For example, suppose that being a three-sided plane figure grounds and explains having interior angles summing to 180°. These properties are necessarily coextensive. Intersubstitution of these necessarily coextensive properties would falsify the claim.

Despite the common view that in order to be explanatory grounding must exhibit asymmetry, irreflexivity, and transitivity, various apparent counter-examples to these three properties of grounding have been proposed.[10] After briefly introducing the most compelling of these examples, I argue that Aristotle, whose theory of ontological priority has been the inspiration for current

---

Trogdon (2021), and Wilson (2018) have argued that grounding is best understood as being explanatory. Glazier (2020) and Wang (2020) outline various forms that such a position has taken. Thompson (2016a) and Wilson (2014), who allege that there are cases of symmetric and reflexive grounding, respectively, unsurprisingly also believe that there is little hope for drawing helpful connections between grounding and explanation, which latter, as they acknowledge, is standardly regarded as asymmetric and irreflexive. Bliss (2018) and Thompson (2018) contend that grounding can be viewed as explanatory provided that explanation can be reflexive and symmetric, respectively. Kovacs (2022, n. 37) observes that those who deny that grounding is asymmetric, irreflexive, or transitive "don't deny the alignment between the formal properties of grounding and those of metaphysical explanation; they seem to be revisionary about both in the same way." Maurin (2019) argues that we cannot infer grounding's features in general from explanation's features in a way that would, independently of other considerations, suffice to justify grounding as an indispensable posit. Skiles and Trogdon (2021) reply. Nolan (in press) argues that grounding's explanatoriness does not entail that grounding is the only metaphysically explanatory notion.

10 Thompson (2020) offers a useful summary of these examples.

interest in grounding,[11] (1) is committed to the asymmetry, irreflexivity, and transitivity of ontological priority, (2) insists in numerous cases that one thing is ontologically prior to another even though it apparently fails to meet his conditions for ontological priority, and (3) provides the materials to reconstruct a unified, principled way of addressing these cases that explains why such (merely) apparent contradictions are ubiquitous. I end by showing how an analog of this Aristotelian response provides a unified, principled answer to the most compelling recent challenges to grounding's status as a strict partial order and clarify an Aristotelian commitment that current advocates of grounding would have to accept in order to adopt such a response. Another way of stating my thesis is this: Recent challenges to the idea that grounding induces a strict partial order on its domain require the truth of a principle that Aristotle requires to be false, on pain of ubiquitous instances in which something is and is not prior to another thing on his view, and Aristotle gives us the resources both to see why the principle should be expected to generate ubiquitous contradictions and to clarify what we would need to believe in order to deny the principle.

2 Challenges to Grounding as Inducing a Strict Partial Order

Those who challenge the asymmetry of grounding think that in certain cases x grounds y and yet y grounds x. The most compelling cases involve parts and wholes. Naomi Thompson (2016b, 2018) provides the following: A circle grounds the semicircles that it comprises and yet these also ground the circle. The circle would not be without them and they would not be without it. Likewise, an organism and its organs ground each other.[12]

---

[11] Fine (1995) and Schaffer (2009) are important in generating the enormous literature on metaphysical dependence and grounding and claim Aristotle's theory of ontological priority as their inspiration. Cameron (2020, p. 49) says that it is "well known that ground has its roots in, broadly speaking, the Aristotelian metaphysical tradition." Corkum (2013b, 2016, 2020) thinks that Aristotle's notion of ontological priority is an important inspiration for current theories of grounding and that attention to such theories is helpful for interpreters of Aristotle. In particular, he highlights that ontological priority and grounding induce strict partial orders on their domain and are explanatory (more specifically, he thinks, such as to back explanations). However, Corkum also cautions against uncritically reading current claims about grounding into ancient texts.

[12] Barnes (2018) might appear to challenge the asymmetry of grounding, but her official position is that although there are no cases in which x and y ground each other, there are cases in which x and y are mutually ontologically dependent. She thinks that ontological dependence is not any sort of relative fundamentality or grounding. As will become clear, I agree at least partially with an analogous version of Barnes's claim that mutual ontological dependence does not entail symmetrical grounding. It is worth noting that Barnes's denial of this entailment is anticipated by Bolzano's (*Wissenschaftslehre* vol. 2, part 3, §202 and §209) denial that mutual determination entails symmetrical grounding. Berker (2018, 757 n. 26) submits that although "Barnes

An alleged counterexample to the claim that grounding is irreflexive is offered by Carrie Jenkins (2011). She thinks that a subject's brain state grounds the subject's pain but is also identical with the subject's pain.

A series of examples that challenge the transitivity of grounding is presented by Jonathan Schaffer (2012). (The name, one-sentence preliminary stipulation, and text of the items for each example are quotations from Schaffer.) For each example, Schaffer thinks that the first two claims are true, but the third, which would be true if grounding were transitive, is false.

THE DENTED SPHERE Imagine a slightly imperfect sphere, with a minor dent.

1 The fact that the thing has a dent grounds the fact that the thing has shape S
2 The fact that the thing has shape S grounds the fact that it is more-or-less spherical
3 The fact that the thing has a dent grounds the fact that it is more-or-less spherical

THE THIRD MEMBER Let S be a set with exactly three members, a, b, and c: $S = \{a, b, c\}$.

1 The fact that c is a member of S grounds the fact that S has exactly three members
2 The fact that S has exactly three members grounds the fact that S has finitely many members
3 The fact that c is a member of S grounds the fact that S has finitely many members

THE CAT'S MEOW Imagine that Cadmus the cat is meowing.

1 The fact that the creature was produced from the meeting of this sperm and that ovum grounds the fact that Cadmus is meowing
2 The fact that Cadmus is meowing grounds the fact that something is meowing
3 The fact that the creature was produced from the meeting of this sperm and that ovum grounds the fact that something is meowing

---

only officially argues that her examples feature instances of mutual *ontological dependence*, not that they feature instances of mutual *grounding* … most of her examples, if they do indeed involve the former, can also be interpreted as involving the latter." I agree at least partially with Barnes's official distinction, but I think that one contribution of my argument is to highlight Aristotelian examples of mutual ontological independence that do not have the problematic feature that Berker identifies for Barnes's examples. An upshot is that Aristotle's account, as I describe it, contradicts Schnieder's (2020, p. 97) claim that "Dependence is the converse of priority" and Beere's (2009, pp. 298–299) claim that in Aristotle's *Categories* and *Metaphysics* ontological priority is the converse of ontological dependence.

Schaffer's intuition is that in each example the first claim features a counterfactual difference-making that the third claim lacks, and that the second claim in each example features either a relationship of determinate to determinable (⊖2 and ^{ABc}2) or a factual witness for an existential generalization (🐈2).

These putative counterexamples to the claim that grounding is asymmetric, irreflexive, and transitive threaten grounding's intuitive status as inducing a strict partial order on its domain. There are other putative counterexamples that, for principled reasons, I do not address. Some involve truth-makers. These are given by Tahko (2013) and Rodriguez-Pereyra (2015). They are less worrying than the examples that I address since some, such as Audi (2020), Fine (2012, pp. 43–46), and Raven (2013, p. 194), contend that truth-making is not a species of grounding. Some of their reasons for thinking not are as follows: Truth-making, unlike grounding, cannot be non-vacuously transitive since truth-making does not admit chains in the first place. It is also too restrictive about the relata since truth-making requires that the first and second relatum be of different types: a worldly first relatum and a representational second relatum. Grounding does not require this and indeed might not permit it. Thompson (2020, pp. 263–264) offers further reasons for resisting the examples given by Tahko and Rodriguez-Pereyra. Other examples that I will not address are given by Bliss (2014, p. 248; 2018, p. 73) of the two poles of a magnet as symmetrical grounds, by Thompson (2018) of the mass, density, and volume of a homogenous fluid as symmetrical grounds, and by Bliss (2018, pp. 82–84) and Wilson (2014, pp. 571–572) of God's existence as a reflexive ground. Like Bennett (2017, p. 37), I suspect that these are best described as cases of having a third (or fourth) thing as a common ground and of either not requiring a ground or being grounded in a complicated way, respectively. Finally, there are alleged examples of symmetrical grounding that involve scenarios the conceivability and metaphysical possibility of which is controversial: Nolan (2018) gives two examples in which one and the same grounding relation is purportedly symmetrical. In one, he imagines a universe that is a proper part of another universe that in its turn is a proper part of the first universe. Another involves a divine being that is a proper part of everything in the totality and is itself the totality. Such cases invite us, as Nolan points out, to reflect on whether they are conceivable in some sense, on the relationship between conceivability and metaphysical possibility, on whether conceivability rather than metaphysical possibility might be appropriate for analysis of the order-theoretic properties of grounding, and on whether an adequate theory of grounding can exclude exotic cases in a principled way.

3 Aristotelian Ontological Priority

Aristotle, whose notion of ontological priority is widely regarded as the inspiration for recent discussions of metaphysical grounding,[13] is committed to ontological priority being asymmetric, irreflexive, and transitive. After establishing this, I will enumerate various cases in which Aristotle insists that one thing is ontologically prior to another and yet apparently fails to meet his conditions for priority. These cases raise what I will refer to as the "Priority Problem," of which I later provide a more exact formulation. This problem is basically that Aristotle apparently thinks that there are cases in which, for some x and some y, x is prior to y and x and y are mutually ontologically dependent, with the result that x can be without y (because of the priority of x to y) and that x cannot be without y (because of their mutual ontological dependence), which would be a contradiction. I will then argue that these numerous apparent contradictions are merely apparent. This solution to the Priority Problem is characteristically Aristotelian, depending only on a distinction often drawn in his works. Nonetheless, showing persuasively that the Priority Problem is merely apparent because of the availability of this particular solution is a nontrivial undertaking. Indeed, the large secondary literature on Aristotle's theory of ontological priority has never produced a systematic way of accounting for the range of Aristotle's examples of ontological priority that I here discuss, or an explanation for the ubiquity of their peculiar structure, both of which would seem desirable to do whether or not the examples are regarded as even *prima facie* problematic. In addition to its importance for absolving Aristotle of what would otherwise be a serious and widespread problem, the solution to the Priority Problem turns out to be useful for addressing alleged failures of the asymmetry, irreflexivity, and transitivity of grounding. In other words, I intend to argue that a standard Aristotelian distinction allows us, for the first time, to account systematically for the range of examples of ontological priority that he discusses, as well as the ubiquity of their peculiar structure, and to circumvent a

---

[13] On the content and importance of Aristotle's theory, see for example Ainsworth (2018), Beere (2009, pp. 293–324), Cleary (1988), Corkum (2008, 2013b, 2016, 2020), Dancy (1981), Edelhoff (2020), Katz (2017), Koslicki (2018, pp. 139–141), Lederman (2014), Makin (2003), Malink (2020), Meadows (2023), Panayides (1999), Peramatzis (2008, 2011), Sirkel (2024), Spellman (1995), and Witt (1994). Corkum (2013b, 2016, 2020), Malink (2020), and Peramatzis (2011) have been most explicit about the connection between Aristotle's notion of ontological priority and current conceptions of grounding, particularly with respect to its asymmetry, irreflexivity, and transitivity. They do not discuss the apparent problem for Aristotle that I describe, but the solution that I offer on Aristotle's behalf is a vindication of their attribution to him of the view that ontological priority, like grounding, is asymmetric, irreflexive, and transitive (i.e., that it induces a strict partial order on its domain).

merely apparent problem for Aristotle raised by those examples. To the extent that the way of avoiding this problem is obvious, it should appear similarly obvious as a solution to a closely analogous problem discussed extensively in current literature on metaphysical grounding, but it has not been recognized.

3.1 Situating Ontological Priority

Before spelling out the Priority Problem for Aristotle, I want both to situate his notion of ontological priority within his discussions of priority in general and to note that his claims about ontological priority have been understood in multiple ways. Aristotle systematically discusses priority in *Categories* 12 and *Metaphysics* 5.11. In the former chapter, Aristotle distinguishes five ways in which one thing can be prior to another:

Temporal priority Priority in time (e.g., older is prior to younger)

Implicative priority Priority in non-reciprocal implication of being (e.g., two implies the being of one but not vice versa)

Positional priority Priority in arrangement (e.g., elements are prior to diagrams, the proëm is prior to the main narrative)

Axiological priority Priority in value (e.g., someone loved more has priority over someone loved less)

Explanatory priority Priority in causation/explanation where implication of being is reciprocal (e.g., Man/a man/a man's being/that there is a man is prior to a true *logos* concerning him/it)

Metaphysics 5.11 features the following taxonomy of the ways in which one thing can be prior to another:

Positional priority Nearer some starting point that is specified absolutely and by nature or relatively

1. Place (closer to the specified spatial starting point)
2. Time (further from now for past events, closer to now for future events)
3. Change (closer to the starting point of change)
4. Capacity (more capable of initiating change)
5. Arrangement (e.g., the person second to the leader of a chorus is prior to the person third from the leader)

Cognitive priority Prior in cognition

1. Account (what is clearer and more intelligible in its own right, e.g., the universal is prior to the particular)

2. Perception (what is clearer and more intelligible from the point of view of our perception, e.g., the particular is prior to the universal)

Derivative priority Prior as a property of what is prior (e.g., straightness of lines is prior to smoothness of surfaces since lines are prior to surfaces)

Ontological priority Prior in nature and substance

1. Categorial (substance, as subject, is prior to …)
2. Potentiality (e.g., matter is prior to substance, part is prior to whole)
3. Actuality (e.g., substance is prior to matter, whole is prior to part)

Various questions arise about how these taxonomies relate to each other. In *Cat.* 12 he says that priority in time is priority in the most dominant sense (*kuriōtata*), whereas he is standardly interpreted as claiming in *Metaph.* 5.11 that all of the listed ways of being prior can in a way be referred to priority in nature and substance, that is, ontological priority ($1019^a11–14$).[14] These claims are easily reconciled, though. In *Cat.* 12 he presumably does not mean that temporal priority is the sense of priority to which the others are focally related, for it is difficult to see how that could be so, but rather that it is the kind of priority that is clearest and most intelligible to us, even if it is not clearest and most intelligible by nature.[15]

Of most importance for present purposes is ontological priority in *Metaph.* 5.11 and whatever it might correspond to in *Cat.* 12. (I will say more about *Cat.* 12 in what follows.) In *Metaph.* 5.11 he attributes the description of this sort of priority to Plato. Here is how Aristotle describes it:[16]

Things are prior in nature and substance that can be without the others, while these cannot be without the former.	τὰ δὲ κατὰ φύσιν καὶ οὐσίαν, ὅσα ἐνδέχεται εἶναι ἄνευ ἄλλων, ἐκεῖνα δὲ ἄνευ ἐκείνων μή·

Metaph. 5.11, $1019^a2–4$[17]

What in *Cat.* 12, if anything, corresponds to this kind of priority? Implicative priority and explanatory priority are the most promising candidates. Unfortunately, the examples that Aristotle offers in explaining them are underspecified,

---

[14] The standard interpretation is adopted by, for example, Bodéüs (2001, p. 151), Cleary (1988, p. 156), (Kirwan, 1971, p. 156), Reeve (2016, p. 370), and Ross (1924, p. 317) but rejected by Peramatzis (2011, pp. 318–319).

[15] This is how Philoponus (*In cat.* 191.24–26) takes it.

[16] All translations are mine from the Oxford Classical Texts unless otherwise noted.

[17] Like most interpreters, I take it that Aristotle speaks in his own voice here, indicating at least partial agreement with Plato. See, for example, Beere (2009, p. 294), Corkum (2008, p. 69), Fine (1984, pp. 35–36), Katz (2017, p. 27), Makin (2003, p. 210), Peramatzis (2011, p. 204), Ross (1924, p. 316), Spellman (1995, p. 8), and Witt (1994, p. 216). One who does not assume this is unlikely to see Aristotle as the kind of inspiration for metaphysical grounding that recent metaphysicians have taken him to be.

leaving open various possible interpretations of what kinds of priority these are, how they relate to each other, and how they relate to ontological priority from *Metaph.* 5.11. Here are Aristotle's descriptions of implicative priority and explanatory priority from *Cat.* 12.

Implicative priority

Second, that which does not reciprocate in implication of being is prior, as one is to two. For from the being of two the being of one follows directly, while from the being of one the being of two does not necessarily follow, so that the implication of being from one to the rest does not reciprocate, and that from which the implication of being is not reciprocal is thought to be prior.

δεύτερον δὲ τὸ μὴ ἀντιστρέφον κατὰ τὴν τοῦ εἶναι ἀκολούθησιν, οἷον τὸ ἓν τῶν δύο πρότερον· δυεῖν μὲν γὰρ ὄντων ἀκολουθεῖ εὐθὺς τὸ ἓν εἶναι, ἑνὸς δὲ ὄντος οὐκ ἀναγκαῖον δύο εἶναι, ὥστε οὐκ ἀντιστρέφει ἀπὸ τοῦ ἑνὸς ἡ ἀκολούθησις τοῦ εἶναι τὸ λοιπόν, πρότερον δὲ δοκεῖ τὸ τοιοῦτον εἶναι ἀφ' οὗ μὴ ἀντιστρέφει ἡ τοῦ εἶναι ἀκολούθησις.

Cat. 12, 14ᵃ29–35

The passage describing explanatory priority has so many interpretive variables that I have left several words in (transliterated) Greek in order to reduce clutter while indicating the possibilities. These words are '*aition*' (cause, explanation, reason), '*anthropos*' (the species Man, an individual man), '*logos*' (account, definition, sentence, statement), and '*pragma*' (thing, fact, state of affairs).

Explanatory priority

There would seem to be another way of being prior beyond those mentioned, for, among things that reciprocate in implication of being, that which is in whatever way the *aition* of the other's being would suitably be labeled prior in nature. It is clear that there are some such cases, for the being of *anthropos* reciprocates in implication of being with the true *logos* of/about it/him. For if *anthropos* is, the *logos* according to which we say that *anthropos* is is true. And indeed this reciprocates, – for if the *logos* according to which we say that *anthropos* is is true, *anthropos* is – but

δόξειε δ' ἂν καὶ παρὰ τοὺς εἰρημένους ἕτερος εἶναι προτέρου τρόπος· τῶν γὰρ ἀντιστρεφόντων κατὰ τὴν τοῦ εἶναι ἀκολούθησιν τὸ αἴτιον ὁπωσοῦν θατέρῳ τοῦ εἶναι πρότερον εἰκότως φύσει λέγοιτ' ἄν. ὅτι δ' ἔστι τινὰ τοιαῦτα, δῆλον· τὸ γὰρ εἶναι ἄνθρωπον ἀντιστρέφει κατὰ τὴν τοῦ εἶναι ἀκολούθησιν πρὸς τὸν ἀληθῆ περὶ αὐτοῦ λόγον· εἰ γὰρ ἔστιν ἄνθρωπος, ἀληθὴς ὁ λόγος ᾧ λέγομεν ὅτι ἔστιν ἄνθρωπος· καὶ ἀντιστρέφει γε, — εἰ γὰρ ἀληθὴς ὁ λόγος ᾧ λέγομεν ὅτι ἔστιν ἄνθρωπος, ἔστιν ἄνθρωπος — ἔστι δὲ ὁ μὲν ἀληθὴς λόγος οὐδαμῶς

<table>
<tr><td>

while the true *logos* is in no way the *aition* of the being of the *pragma*, the *pragma* seems in some way the *aition* of the *logos* being a true one. For in virtue of the *pragma* being, the *logos* is labeled true or false.

</td><td>

αἴτιος τοῦ εἶναι τὸ πρᾶγμα, τὸ μέντοι πρᾶγμα φαίνεταί πως αἴτιον τοῦ εἶναι ἀληθῆ τὸν λόγον· τῷ γὰρ εἶναι τὸ πρᾶγμα ἢ μὴ ἀληθὴς ὁ λόγος ἢ ψευδὴς λέγεται.

</td></tr>
</table>

Cat. 12, 14^{b}10–22

In order briefly to outline typical ways of understanding these descriptions of priority and how they relate to each other, it will be helpful to introduce a distinction that has been important in recent literature on Aristotle's theory of priority between different ways of construing ontological priority:[18]

Existential priority For all x and all y, x is existentially ontologically prior to y if and only if x can exist without y existing but y cannot exist without x existing.

Essential priority For all x and all y, x is essentially ontologically prior to y if and only if x can be what x is without y being what y is but y cannot be what y is without x being what x is.

Ontic priority For all x and all y, x is ontically prior to y if and only if x has the ontological status of a being independently of standing in some tie to y, but y has its ontological status in virtue of (that is to say, grounded in) standing in a tie to x.

Fine (1995, p. 271) offers a couple of examples that bring out the difference between the kinds of ontological dependence encoded in the formulations of existential priority, on the one hand, and essential and ontic priority, on the other: Socrates is essentially and ontically prior to his singleton, {Socrates}, but is not existentially prior to it since these exist in the same possible worlds. The number 2 is existentially prior to Socrates, since unlike Socrates it necessarily exists, but it is not essentially or ontically prior to Socrates since what it is to be Socrates does not depend on what it is to be the number 2 and neither does Socrates' ontological status as a being depend on that of the number 2. In addition, Fine (1995, p. 271) points out that the existential construal overgenerates dependence relations, since any contingent thing will depend on any necessary thing. These and other considerations are leveraged by, for example, Corkum (2008, 2013b, 2016, 2020) and Peramatzis (2008, 2011) to argue against the

---

[18] For the first, see especially Fine (1984) and for the second see especially Peramatzis (2008, 2011). In the case of the third, the description, but not the label, is adapted from Corkum (2008, 2013b, 2020) and especially Corkum (2016, p. 8).

general appropriateness of existential priority for capturing Aristotle's notion of ontological priority.

One way in which this distinction matters is that if grounding is, as most recent authors think (see p. 4 n. 9), explanatory, and essential and ontic priority are, as their advocates think, explanatory, then existential priority is less like grounding than essential and ontic priority are.[19] That is because existential priority requires no explanatory connection between prior and posterior items. Those who think that Aristotle's notion of ontological priority is existential priority and concur with the majority opinion that grounding is explanatory will therefore be correspondingly less inclined to see Aristotle's notion as relevant to recent discussions of the problems and prospects of grounding. One might think, of course, that for Aristotle ontological priority is sometimes existential priority and sometimes essential or ontic priority, or that it is at least sometimes to be construed in some other way. My argument does not require taking a position on this issue. However, I think that whether or not Aristotelian ontological priority is ever essential or ontic priority, it is always explanatory in some way or other.

There might initially appear to be two exceptions to the explanatoriness of Aristotelian ontological priority, both of which Malink (2013, pp. 356–358) regards as problematic for Peramatzis's (2011) claim about the nature of the explanatory relationship between prior and posterior things. Peramatzis thinks that Aristotle countenances the following criterion for ontological priority: If x is ontologically prior to y then x is included in the account of y's essence, but not vice versa, and thus at least partially explains what it is to be y. My proposal, which is compatible with, but weaker than, Peramatzis's, is simply that all of Aristotle's claims of ontological priority introduce a context of *per se* explanatory relevance. The first problem that Malink discusses for Peramatzis, as does Meadows (2023), is one that Peramatzis anticipates (pp. 296–299), namely that eternal things are prior to perishable things (*Metaph.* 9.8, 1050^b6–1051^a3). Malink and Meadows argue, against Peramatzis, that eternal things are not part of the essence of perishable things. Even if they are not parts of their essence, though, eternal things are explanatory of perishable things in at least the following ways, the second of which Peramatzis (2011, p. 298) mentions: The sun's eternal motion on an inclined circle (in turn explained by other eternal things) at least partially explains the generation and perishing

---

[19] There are, of course, other reasons why this distinction matters for Aristotle, even outside the context of *Categories* and *Metaphysics*. For the applicability of the distinction between existential and essential priority to various claims in Aristotle's ethical theory, for example, see Reece (2023, 40 and ch. 5).

of terrestrial things (*Phys.* 2.2, 194^{b}13; *GC* 2.10, 336^{a}23–^{b}12; *Metaph.* 12.5, 1071^{a}15, 12.6, 1072^{a}3–18, 12.10, 1075^{b}24–25) and the elements mentioned in citing material causes of perishable things have tendencies that are explained by their imitation of eternal, celestial things (*Metaph.* 9.8, 1050^{b}28–29; *GC* 1.3; *Metaph.* 12.5–7). (I do not mean to suggest that such considerations are Aristotle's only, or even primary, points of reference in his argument for the priority of eternal to perishable things in the context of *Metaph.* 9.8 itself; my point is rather that, according to him, this priority claim does in fact introduce a context of *per se* explanatory relevance, a point for which Meadows argues.) The second is that locomotion is prior to alteration and growth (*Phys.* 8.7, 260^{a}27–^{b}7). Again, Malink contends that locomotion is not part of the essence of other kinds of change. Even so, locomotion partially explains them, according to Aristotle, since locomotion is involved in affection and affection is involved in growth.

The distinction between existential priority, on the one hand, and essential and ontic priority, on the other, facilitates taxonomizing different accounts of Aristotle's descriptions of implicative priority and explanatory priority from *Cat.* 12 and ontological priority from *Metaph.* 5.11 and their relationships to each other.[20] Most recent commentators suppose that at least implicative priority from *Cat.* 12 is existential priority. The most frequently voiced disagreement is about whether explanatory priority from that chapter and ontological priority from *Metaph.* 5.11 are existential. Those who regard ontological priority from *Metaph.* 5.11 as essential or ontic priority tend to think that explanatory priority from *Cat.* 12, but not implicative priority, corresponds to it. Those who take ontological priority from *Metaph.* 5.11 to be existential priority, by contrast, suppose that implicative priority, but not explanatory priority, from *Cat.* 12 corresponds to it.

Some implications of the distinction between existential and essential priority can be appreciated by rehearsing some different ways of describing the example that he uses to illustrate implicative priority from *Cat.* 12. On one reading, Aristotle means that if two things exist, then it follows that (at least) one thing exists, but from the claim that one thing exists it does not follow that two things exist. On another reading, he means that if the number two exists, then it

---

[20] Such accounts are available in, e.g., Ackrill (1963, pp. 111–112), Beere (2009, p. 294 n. 14, pp. 298–299), Bodéüs (2001, p. 66), Cleary (1988, pp. 25–29), Corkum (2008, pp. 72–76), Crivelli (2004, p. 104), Edelhoff (2020, pp. 27–31), Katz (2017, pp. 33–38), Kirwan (1971, p. 153), Meadows (2023, p. 208), Mesquita (2025, pp. 31–36), Oehler (2006, pp. 339–343), Panayides (1999, p. 342), Peramatzis (2008, p. 204 n. 24; 2011, pp. 235–244), Ross (1924^b vol. 1, p. 317), Sirkel (2024), and Zanatta (1989, pp. 674–679).

follows that the number one exists, but not vice versa. This, though, is implausible if numbers exist necessarily. More likely, if the numbers one and two are at issue, is that he means that what it is to be one is included in what it is to be two ("and the rest"), but not vice versa. In other words, the essence-specifying definition of the number one figures in the essence-specifying definition of the number two, but not vice versa. Some evidence that Aristotle has this in mind is the example that he gives of this kind of priority in the next chapter (as well as *Top.* 4.2, 123^a14–15, and 6.4, 141^b29): The genus Animal is prior to the species Fish, for they do not reciprocate in implication of being.[21] It would be problematic to maintain that a genus can exist without the species under it existing if one thinks, as Aristotle does, that species exist perpetually (*Phys.* 3.6, 206^a25–27; *GA* 2.1, 731^b24–732^a1) and all and only things that exist perpetually exist necessarily (*DC* 1.12; *GC* 2.11). It is likelier that Aristotle means that the genus is part of the definition of the species under it, or in other words, that what it is to be an animal, say, is included in what it is to be a fish, but not vice versa (*Metaph.* 5.25, 1023^b23–25).

The relevance of the genus/species example is interesting for an additional reason, which is also noticed by at least some of the ancient commentators. Consider Aristotle's uses of it in *Cat.* 13 and in *Top.* 4.2, 123^a14–15. In the first, he is discussing simultaneity (the opposite of priority) *in nature*. In the second, he directly labels the kind of priority that genus has to species 'priority in nature.' This is interesting because he also applies that description to explanatory priority from *Cat.* 12, a fact that has tempted some to think that explanatory priority, but not implicative priority, corresponds to priority in nature and substance (ontological priority) from *Metaph.* 5.11. But as we have seen, he thinks that genus is prior in nature to species and that this example illustrates the same kind of priority as does his example of one and two, namely implicative priority from *Cat.* 12. So, the label 'priority in nature' does not align one of these more closely than the other with ontological priority from *Metaph.* 5.11.

As for explanatory priority from *Cat.* 12, even aside from the mysteriousness of the example that Aristotle gives to illustrate it and how it comports with the abstract description and label that he applies to this kind of priority – options are described in the sources referenced in the two preceding footnotes – questions arise about the relevance of causation/explanation. One is this: Does Aristotle mean that *only in*, or *even in*, cases in which the implication

---

[21] Ancient commentators tend either to add this example to that of one and two or to use it exclusively: Alexander of Aphrodisias (*In APr 1* 6.35–7.5, *In top.* 367.16–20), Ammonius (*In cat.* 103.13–18), Olympiodorus (*In cat.* 144.33), Philoponus (*In cat.* 192.14–17), Simplicius (*In cat.* 419.33–420.5), Elias (*In cat.* 251.29), Sergius of Rešᶜainā (*Introduction* §101, *Categories* §440), John of Damascus (*Dialectica* 60.5–11).

of being is reciprocal is priority properly described as causal/explanatory?[22] Since, as we have seen, on at least some plausible construals of examples meant to correspond to implicative priority from *Cat.* 12, one is explanatory of two and genus is explanatory of species, 'even in' seems to be the safer suggestion, as noticed by Simplicius (*In cat.* 421.2). This would leave open the possibility that both implicative priority and explanatory priority in *Cat.* 12 are explanatory. It then becomes somewhat difficult to explain why Aristotle seems to distinguish them. However, as many commentators have noted, he is far from clear about whether explanatory priority is its own kind of priority distinct from each of the other four at all.

On any way of understanding Aristotle's remarks about explanatory priority (if it is its own kind) of priority, it should not turn out both that x is prior in being to y and that the being of x and y are reciprocal, at the same time and in the same respect, if, as I take it, priority is non-reciprocal. After all, if priority were not non-reciprocal, then given the transitivity of priority, which I will show that Aristotle maintains, something could be prior to itself, which he explicitly denies in a passage that I will later discuss (*MA* 5, 700^{b}3): Given transitivity, if x is prior to y and y to z then x is prior to z. On the supposition that priority reciprocates in this case, z is prior to y and y to x, so by transitivity z is prior to x. So, x would be prior to z and z to x, which by transitivity yields that x is prior to x, which Aristotle says is impossible.

It is worth noting that there are at least two relevant variables of 'respect' in 'in the same respect.' One is the meaning of 'being' in the two conjuncts. If for one meaning of 'being' the being of x and y is reciprocal and for another meaning of 'being' the being of x is prior to the being of y, then there is no contradiction.[23] This requires Aristotle to be discussing *two* kinds of ontological relationship (one for each sense of 'being') under this heading.

Some think that Aristotle discusses two kinds of relationship under this heading that are each appropriately called ontological but also that there is only one sense of 'being' at issue.[24] The idea is that the reciprocal relationship is reciprocity in being and the asymmetrical relationship is that of explanatory priority that holds between beings (or between the being of beings). Avoiding contradiction by dissociating ontological priority and explanatory priority in this way, but without this collapsing into other strategies for avoiding contradiction that appeal to the explanatoriness of ontological priority, would require two things:

---

[22] Sirkel (2024, p. 46) raises this question clearly and reports seeing no reason for thinking that Aristotle here means 'only in.'

[23] Such an approach is advocated by Bodéüs (2001, p. 66) and Edelhoff (2020, pp. 27–31).

[24] See, e.g., Cleary (1988, pp. 27–28), Katz (2017, pp. 37–38), Schnieder and Werner (2021, p. 152), and Sirkel (2024, pp. 46–48, 57, 60–61).

First, it would require that explanatory priority is its own kind of priority distinct from the kinds listed in *Cat.* 12, which many have noted is not obviously something that Aristotle believes. Second, it would require that explanatory priority can occur in the absence of *any* kind of ontological priority, whether existential, essential, ontic, *vel sim.*, in cases of the type imagined in *Cat.* 12, which is also not obviously Aristotle's view. Furthermore, even if this strategy works locally for avoiding contradiction as an interpretation of *Cat.* 12, it will not, as I will later show (p. 28), work globally for avoiding contradictions of the same general type that arise in other passages, namely cases in which Aristotle appears to think both that x can be without y being and that x cannot be without y being. If a solution to the local problem involved in interpreting *Cat.* 12 is available that also solves the global problem of avoiding contradictions of the same general type, but without requiring the two controversial commitments that I have just mentioned and without incurring other costs, it should be preferred.[25]

The way of avoiding contradiction that I favor is to leave the meaning of 'being' constant and distinguish between relevant qualifications of x and y: there is some pair of qualifications (one for x and one for y) under which the implication of being is reciprocal and some other pair of qualifications under which the implication of being is asymmetric. This approach is independently motivated by the fact that we need to distinguish pairs of qualifications of x and y anyway in order to account for the applicability of causation/explanation, which Aristotle thinks requires isolating particular qualifications.[26] I will say more in subsequent sections about qualifications and causation/explanation, as well as about the general applicability of this strategy for addressing cases with a structure relevantly similar to that which generates the interpretive problem that I have been discussing for *Cat.* 12.

It is possible to say much more about the details of Aristotle's descriptions of implicative priority and explanatory priority from *Cat.* 12 and ontological priority from *Metaph.* 5.11, as well as about their relationship to each other, but my overall aim in this Element does not require doing so. What is important for my purposes is that all three of these descriptions imply asymmetry and irreflexivity of the kind(s) of priority that they describe. (The description of

---

[25] Thanks to Riin Sirkel for suggesting clarification of the points made in this paragraph.

[26] It is interesting that the advocates of the first of the approaches that I mentioned either do not address the applicability of causation/explanation to this kind of priority, in the case of Bodéüs, or flag it as uncertain and problematic, in the case of Edelhoff. It is also interesting that some current grounding theorists, e.g., deRosett (2023, p. 5) and Schnieder and Werner (2021, p. 152), think that Aristotle's description of this kind of priority is a description of grounding that highlights grounding's explanatoriness.

explanatory priority from *Cat.* 12 implies that even if some reciprocal relation obtains between the things in question, the priority relation that obtains between them is asymmetric.)[27] None is more or less suggestive of transitivity than the others are, though, as I will argue, it is clear that he thinks that ontological priority, like other kinds of priority, is transitive.[28]

3.2 Commitment to ontological priority as inducing a strict partial order

Aristotelian ontological priority, like metaphysical grounding, induces a strict partial order on its domain.

3.2.1 Commitment to Asymmetry

First, as I indicated at the end of the preceding section, Aristotle's implicative priority and explanatory priority from *Cat.* 12, as well as ontological priority from *Metaph.* 5.11, are clearly asymmetric since the implication of being is unidirectional and holds between distinct items. (Again, according to the description of explanatory priority from *Cat.* 12 the *priority* relation does not have convertible terms – one thing is the cause/explanation of the other, *but not vice versa* – even though there is a mutual implication of being in some other respect.)

Furthermore, certain arguments that he makes against separated universals depend on the asymmetry of ontological priority:

But in general the opposite, both of the truth and of what is customarily supposed, follows, if someone thus posits mathematicals to be separated natures. For while if they are such it is necessary	ὅλως δὲ τοὐναντίον συμβαίνει καὶ τοῦ ἀληθοῦς καὶ τοῦ εἰωθότος ὑπολαμβάνεσθαι, εἴ τις θήσει οὕτως εἶναι τὰ μαθηματικὰ ὡς κεχωρισμένας τινὰς φύσεις. ἀνάγκη γὰρ διὰ τὸ μὲν

---

[27] Katz (2017, pp. 37–38) and Sirkel (2024, pp. 46–48, 57, 60–61) express clearly that Aristotle's description of explanatory priority involves two distinct ontological relations, one that is symmetric and another that is asymmetric.

[28] It may be thought that explanatory priority from *Cat.* 12, since the example used to illustrate it features 'true,' is uniquely susceptible to the alleged counterexamples to the asymmetry, irreflexivity, and transitivity of truthmaking propounded by Rodriguez-Pereyra (2015). However, it is controversial whether Aristotle thinks of this kind of priority as truthmaking. It is unclear what role truth plays in his example and whether examples not involving an explicit appeal to truth might meet the description that he gives of this kind of priority. See, e.g., Sirkel (2024, p. 60). Also, even if he does so think of it, his theory of truth does not obviously permit the patterns of existential generalization over propositions or propositional self-reference on which Rodriguez-Pereyra's examples depend. Problems arising from these patterns and possible solutions to them are discussed by, e.g., Correia (2024, pp. 68–78), Fine (2010), Goodman (2023), Korbmacher (2018a, 2018b), and Wilhelm (2021).

<table>
<tr><td>

for these to be prior to perceptible magnitudes, but in truth they are posterior. For an incomplete magnitude is prior in becoming, but posterior in being, such as the inanimate to the animate.

</td><td>

οὕτως εἶναι αὐτὰς προτέρας εἶναι τῶν αἰσθητῶν μεγεθῶν, κατὰ τὸ ἀληθὲς δὲ ὑστέρας· τὸ γὰρ ἀτελὲς μέγεθος γενέσει μὲν πρότερόν ἐστι, τῇ οὐσίᾳ δ' ὕστερον, οἷον ἄψυχον ἐμψύχου.

</td></tr>
</table>

Metaph. 13.2, 1077ª14–20

He can legitimately criticize Platonists in the way that he does only if ontological priority is asymmetric. His criticism is that they take separated mathematicals to be prior to perceptible magnitudes, but in fact perceptible magnitudes are prior. If ontological priority were not asymmetric, though, then it would be open to Platonists to say that this is a case in which the priority runs both directions: Perceptible magnitudes are prior to separated mathematicals, as Aristotle says, *and* posterior to them. Aristotle clearly assumes that this would be incoherent. Furthermore, his assumption does not seem to be specific to this particular case of priority. It is not because of features peculiar to perceptible magnitudes that they cannot be both prior to and posterior to the same thing at the same time in the same respect but rather because of what it means to be prior and what it means to be posterior. After all, he does not bother to defend this part of the argument. If he had meant instead that *in this case in particular* priority does not run in both directions, we would reasonably have expected him to give a reason why it does not do so in this case but does in others. He gives no such reason.[29]

To say that Aristotelian ontological priority is asymmetric is to say that the prior and posterior terms never convert. On Aristotle's account, if x is ontologically prior to y then the following two things are true: x can be without y and y cannot be without x. These would have counterinstances only if ontological priority were not asymmetric (i.e., either not antisymmetric or not irreflexive).

3.2.2 Commitment to Irreflexivity

Aristotle's descriptions of ontological priority that I have just mentioned commit him to the asymmetry of ontological priority and asymmetry entails irreflexivity. In addition, irreflexivity of priority, as for other comparative

---

[29] Thanks to an anonymous reviewer for suggesting discussion of whether this passage shows only that Aristotle thinks that there is at least one case of priority that is not symmetric or instead reveals his willingness to make a more general assumption about priority and posteriority being opposites. I think the latter. The evidential import of this passage for my purposes has nothing to do with what Aristotle is claiming to be prior to what, but rather with its encoding of an assumption without which his argument in the passage, or indeed any structurally analogous argument, would fail.

relations (e.g., *more massive than, further from*, etc.), follows from the indiscernibility of identicals,[30] a principle that Aristotle explicitly endorses in a specific form that I will later discuss (*SE* 24, 179ª37–39; *Phys.* 3.3, 202ᵇ14–16). After all, if x is more massive than y then they do not have the same mass. But supposing that $x = y$, as would be licit if comparative relations in general, or *more massive than* in particular, were not irreflexive, would yield the absurd result that the same thing at the same time has and does not have its particular mass. Furthermore, one might think that irreflexivity is implicit in the way that he introduces ontological priority:

One thing is said to be prior to *another* in four ways.

Πρότερον ἕτερον ἑτέρου λέγεται τετραχῶς·

Cat. 12, 14ª26 (emphasis added)[31]

Unsurprisingly, he owns the commitment to irreflexivity:

It is completely impossible for anything to cause its own generation and corruption. For the mover must be prior to the moved, and the begetter to the begotten, and *nothing can be prior to itself*.

γενέσεως δὲ καὶ φθορᾶς οὐδαμῶς οἷόν τε αὐτὸ αἴτιον εἶναι αὐτῷ οὐθέν. προϋπάρχειν γὰρ δεῖ τὸ κινοῦν τοῦ κινουμένου καὶ τὸ γεννῶν τοῦ γεννωμένου· αὐτὸ δ' αὐτοῦ πρότερον οὐδέν ἐστιν.

MA 5, 700ª35–ᵇ3 (Primavesi ed., emphasis added)

One might think that he is leveraging a point only about temporal priority, not about ontological priority, but this would not make sense of his focus on generation *and* corruption, that is, substantial change in general. Nothing prevents the temporal overlap of mover and moved. Indeed, *qua* mover and moved, they are precisely contemporaneous (*Phys.* 3.1). But any possibility of temporal overlap of corrupter and corrupted would render dubious an assertion that facts about temporal priority are supposed to preclude the possibility of anything being the cause of its own corruption. It would be incoherent, though, to suppose that something could be the cause of its own substantial change if such change requires that thing to be (in order to be what imparts the change) and not to be (at some stage of the process, in order to be what is changed from not being to being or vice versa) and nothing can be ontologically prior to itself.

---

[30] This is mentioned by Bennett (2017, p. 41).

[31] The first-century BC commentator Boethus of Sidon (ap. Simplicius *In cat.* 163.15–29) infers the irreflexivity of relativity from Aristotle's use of '*heterôn*' in his description at *Cat.* 6ª36–37 and is joined by Duncombe (2020, p. 93) in doing so. If they are correct, the same reason would apply to the way in which Aristotle describes ontological priority.

That is Aristotle's point. If he here relies on a commitment to the irreflexivity of ontological priority, a commitment independent from this passage, his argument is more convincing than it would otherwise be.

3.2.3 Commitment to Transitivity

Aristotle assumes the transitivity of ontological priority, relying on it for various arguments. It will be helpful to correlate these with the list of ways of being ontologically prior, that is, prior in nature and substance, in *Metaph.* 5.11. Unlike in the initial presentation of the taxonomy of kinds of priority discussed in that chapter, I here fill in the first way with three claims that Aristotle elsewhere affirms but does not here mention:

1. Categorial (substance, as subject, is prior to…)
    (a) Substance, whether primary or secondary, is prior to other categories of being, such as quantity and quality, and these in turn are prior to correlatives.
    (b) Genus is prior to species as said of them, which in turn is prior to particular substances as said of them.
    (c) Primary substance is more of a substance than species is, which in turn is more of a substance than genus is.
2. Potentiality (e.g., matter is prior to substance, part is prior to whole)
3. Actuality (e.g., substance is prior to matter, whole is prior to part)

Aristotle affirms (1a), thereby assuming transitivity, in *Metaph.* 14.1, $1088^a15–^b4$, where he argues that putative Platonist first principles of being, in particular the great and the small, do not have the ontological fundamentality required of genuine first principles of being. This is, he says, because the great and the small turn out to be correlatives. He offers several interconnected reasons for thinking that their correlativity precludes having the appropriate fundamentality. The one most relevant for my purposes here is that the great and the small, as correlatives, are "least of all a nature or substance" (1088^a23). Far from being principles of substances and other categories of being, such as quantity and quality, correlatives like the great and the small are ontologically posterior to all of these. The reason that Aristotle gives is that they are ontologically posterior to quantity and quality ($1088^a24–25$), which in turn are ontologically posterior to substance (1088^b4). Aristotle is assuming that ontological priority is transitive. Another way to put this point is that it is clearly important to Aristotle in this passage that correlatives are the *least* substantial of the categories. This implies an ordering: Substance is the most substantial, some categories of being are less substantial than substance is, and correlatives, being less substantial than those are, are the least substantial of any of the categories of being. An ordering relation of this kind is transitive, as well as asymmetric and irreflexive.

Claims (1b) and (1c) might, as some commentators think, simply amount to instances of (2) and (3). In any case, Aristotle affirms (1b) in *Cat.* 3, $1^b 10$–15 and (1c) in *Cat.* 5, $2^b 7$–21. The examples in both passages feature the genus Animal, the species Man, and individual humans: Animal is said of Man and therefore of individual humans. Individual humans are substances most of all and the species Man is more of a substance than the genus Animal is. Aristotle's commitment to transitivity, as well as to asymmetry and irreflexivity, is here evident.

Aristotle also assumes the transitivity of ontological priority in accordance with (2) in *Phys.* 8.7, $260^a 27$–$^b 7$, where he contends that locomotion is prior to affection and growth. His strategy is to argue that locomotion is required for affection and affection is required for growth. He concludes from this that locomotion is therefore required for growth, too, but he could not do so unless priority is transitive. The kind of priority discussed in these lines is not temporal priority, as we can tell from the fact that he distinguishes temporal priority as a separate kind and goes on to argue later in the chapter that locomotion is *also* temporally prior to affection and growth ($260^b 29$). The latter argument, unsurprisingly, depends on points about temporal ordering, but the former argument does not do so. Rather, it depends on claims about what locomotion, affection, and growth involve. Locomotion is prior to the other two because it is involved in, and therefore presupposed by, them. *This* argument, then, is not one for locomotion's temporal priority, for that comes later, but rather for its ontological priority, as Graham (1999, p. 126) avers.

He also assumes that the ontological priority of wholes to parts, (3) above, is transitive in *Pol.* 1.2, $1253^a 18$–1.3, $1253^b 8$: States are ontologically prior to individuals because states are prior to families, families are prior to individuals, families are parts of states, individuals are parts of families, and wholes are prior to parts. This argument fails if the ontological priority of wholes to parts is not transitive.

For each type of example of ontological priority that he taxonimizes in *Metaph.* 5.11, then, Aristotle assumes transitivity, on pain of the failure of arguments featuring examples of these types. As in my discussion of his assumption of the asymmetry of ontological priority, it is the role of the assumption itself in these arguments that is of interest; there is no reason to think that the assumption depends on features peculiar to the examples.

It is hardly surprising that Aristotle takes ontological priority to be asymmetric, irreflexive, and transitive. He clearly regards the other kinds of priority that he discusses as having these order-theoretic properties. The more obvious cases are priority in place, time, change, arrangement, and value. Even the less obvious kinds, like cognitive priority, induce strict partial orders on their domains (*Phys.* 5.3, 227^{a}17–22, 8.7, 261^{a}10–^{b}15; *Metaph.* 2.1, 994^{a}10–16).[32] One might attempt to argue that ontological priority is unlike the other kinds of priority in this respect. That is implausible, though, since apart from their being referred somehow to ontological priority as the central case of priority, which, as I have already said, Aristotle is standardly interpreted as asserting at *Metaph.* 5.11, 1019^{a}11–12, there is not much to relate the numerous kinds of priority other than their inducing strict partial orders on their domains.[33]

3.3 The Priority Problem

According to Aristotle's description of ontological priority, if x is ontologically prior to y then both of the following are true:

1. x can be without y
2. y cannot be without x

But according to him there are cases in which, apparently, x is ontologically prior to y, but x and y are mutually ontologically dependent, or as Aristotle says, "correlatives" (*ta pros ti*).

Correlatives "those things for which being is the same as being somehow related to something" (*Cat.* 7, 8^{a}31–32)

Standard examples of correlatives include:

- double and half
- larger and smaller
- knowledge and knowable
- perception and perceptible
- mover and moved

---

[32] It is possible that the kind of priority at issue in Aristotle's theory of demonstration in *Posterior Analytics* is a kind of ontological priority. Aristotle calls it "priority in nature" as opposed to "priority in relation to us," viewing this distinction as isomorphic with the distinction between "more known by nature" and "more known in relation to us" (1.2, 71^{b}33–72^{a}5). Malink (2020, pp. 39–44) shows that this kind of priority in nature is asymmetric, irreflexive, and transitive, citing 1.3, 72^{b}27–8 and 2.16, 98^{b}16–21 in support, and argues that it can be understood as a kind of grounding relation. Bolzano (1837, part 3, §209), on the basis of the first of these passages, says that Aristotle here describes grounding, that it is asymmetric, and that he has the same thing in mind in *Cat.* 12.

[33] Noticing that the various kinds of priority are related in this way, as did Sebastián Izquierdo (*PS* disp. 15, q. 7), is an interesting upshot of the kind of order-theoretic investigation encouraged by attention to recent problems posed for the notion of grounding. Thanks to an anonymous reviewer for this point.

He thinks that all correlatives convert (*antistrephein*), that is, that they are such that x is correlative to y if and only if y is correlative to x (*Cat.* 7, 6^{b}28–7^{b}14). According to him, correlatives are such that neither can be without the other.[34] So, if x and y are correlatives then both of the following are true:

1. x cannot be without y
2. y cannot be without x

Now we can state the Priority Problem:

Priority Problem If Aristotle thinks that there are cases in which, for some x and some y, x is prior to y and x and y are correlatives, then it would be true both that x can be without y (because of the priority of x to y) and that x cannot be without y (because of their correlativity), which would be a contradiction. He appears to think that there are such cases.

In other words, the problem is that, apparently, there are cases in which Aristotle insists that ontological priority obtains, but one of his conditions for priority is not met.[35] In the following cases it might appear that Aristotle devolves into incoherence by saying both that the first item is prior to the second and that they are correlatives:

- knowable and knowledge
  - knowable is prior to knowledge (*Cat.* 7, 7^{b}23–24)
  - knowable and knowledge are correlatives (*Metaph.* 5.15, 1021^{a}29–30)
- perceptible and perception
  - perceptible is prior to perception (*Metaph.* 4.5, 1010^{b}35–1011^{a}2)
  - perceptible and perception are correlatives (*Cat.* 7, 7^{b}36 8^{a}11–12, *DA* 1.1, 402^{b}15–16)
- thinkable and thought
  - thinkable is prior to thought (*DA* 2.4, 415^{a}17–22)

---

[34] For in-depth discussion of Aristotle's theory of correlatives, see Ackrill (1963, pp. 98–103), Duncombe (2015, 2020), Edelhoff (2020), Gottlieb (1993), Harari (2011), Hood (2004), Kelsey (2022, ch. 5), Mesquita (2025), Mignucci (1986), Morales (1994), Oehler (2006, pp. 292–313), Reece (2024, pp. 18–20; ms-b), and Sedley (2002).

[35] Peramatzis (2011, p. 168) describes and attempts to resolve a tension that is related to, but stronger than, the Priority Problem. Peramatzis, like Charles (2021), thinks that the tension is that forms are essentially enmattered, but this is difficult to square with their priority to matter. I am not committed to the claim that, for Aristotle, forms are essentially enmattered. However, a claim that Peramatzis and Charles consider evidence for that view, namely the claim that the form and matter of natural objects are correlatives, would be, in combination with Aristotle's insistence that form is ontologically prior to matter, enough to generate the Priority Problem without requiring their further claim, criticized by Corkum (2013a), Malink (2013), and Meister (2020), that form is essentially enmattered. Peramatzis and Charles do not thematize the problem in full generality, focusing rather on the example of form and matter. (Thanks to both of them for helpful discussion of these issues.)

- thinkable and thought are correlatives (*DA* 1.1, 402^{b}15–16, *Metaph.* 5.15, 1021^{a}29–30)
- objects of psychic activities and those activities
  - objects of psychic activities are prior to those activities (*DA* 2.4, 415^a 14–22)
  - psychic activities and their objects are correlatives (*DA* 2.4, 415^{a}20)[36]
- what acts upon something and that upon which it acts
  - what acts upon something is prior to that upon which it acts (*Metaph.* 4.5, 1010^{b}37–1011^{a}1, 5.15, 1021^{a}22–25)
  - what acts upon something and that upon which it acts are correlatives (*Phys.* 3.1, 200^{b}28–32)
- the form of a natural object and its matter
  - the form of a natural object is prior to its matter (*Metaph.* 7.10, 1035^{b}11– 21, 9.8, 1050^{a}4–16)
  - the form and matter of a natural object are correlatives (*Phys.* 2.2, 194^{b}8)[37]
- monad and dyad
  - monad is prior to dyad (*Cat.* 12, 14^{a}29–35)
  - monad and dyad are correlatives (*Cat.* 7, 6^{a}39)
- circle and semicircle
  - circle is prior to semicircle (*Metaph.* 7.10, 1035^{b}9–11)
  - circle and semicircle are correlatives (*Cat.* 7, 6^{a}39)

One might be tempted to think that it would be unproblematic for x to be ontologically prior to y and for x and y to be correlatives if y is correlative to x but x is not correlative to y. Some interpreters attribute to Aristotle the view that there are "non-simultaneous" (*ouk hama*) correlatives that satisfy this description, on the strength of *Cat.* 7, 7^{b}22–24.

But it is far from obvious that Aristotle believes that there are non-simultaneous correlatives. He there uses 'seems' ('*dokei*') in the first clause and 'would seem' ('*an doxeien*') in the second, and while such terms do not always dissociate him from the position in question, their use leaves open the possibility that he regards apparent examples of non-simultaneous correlatives as merely apparent.

Indeed, the ancient commentators on this passage think that he so regards them, in part for the reason that the appearance of non-simultaneity depends

---

[36] The word that Aristotle uses here is '*antikeimena*' (opposites), here clearly meaning *correlative* opposites, rather than one of the other kinds of opposites distinguished in *Cat.* 10 and *Metaph.* 5.10.

[37] Charles (2021, 43 n. 1, 45) discusses the correlativity of the form of a natural object and its matter with reference to these passages.

on failing to hold constant the potentiality or actuality of both correlatives.[38] Another reason, discussed by Alexander of Aphrodisias (*In top.* 384.4–12, 441.5–20) and Simplicius (*In cat.* 194.32–195.30), is that Aristotle says that opposites, the genus of which correlatives are a species, are simultaneous by nature (*Top.* 5.3, 131ª14–16, 6.4, 142ª24).[39]

Even if proponents of non-simultaneous correlatives were correct, though, only some of the apparently problematic examples would count as non-simultaneous correlatives on their view. What acts and that upon which it acts must be simultaneous correlatives, for Aristotle, and likewise for monad and dyad and circle and semicircle since double and half are uncontroversial examples of simultaneous correlatives. So, the Priority Problem would remain.

Similarly, one might wonder whether the dependence between correlatives could in each of these cases be an unproblematic mutual existential dependence. I would not want to commit to that if another way of addressing these examples can possibly be found. That is because it is controversial whether *any* of these examples is one of mutual existential, *but not* essential or ontic, dependence.

One might also wonder whether apparently problematic cases of correlatives for which one is prior to the other could be addressed by appealing to the distinction, mentioned earlier, between ontological priority understood existentially, on the one hand, and essentially or ontically, on the other. But the distinction addresses such cases only if it allows us to show that for every apparently problematic case the priority is only existential and the correlativity only essential or ontic, or the priority only essential or ontic and the correlativity only existential. It cannot do so. Here is why: All properly specified correlatives have mutually dependent essences (*Cat.* 7, 8ª31–32), and so are mutually essentially dependent and mutually ontically dependent, all simultaneous correlatives are mutually existentially dependent, and even if Aristotle positively commits to the existence of non-simultaneous correlatives, which I have just said is far from obvious, several of the examples of correlatives that I have cited as apparently threatening the asymmetry of priority are clearly simultaneous correlatives.

Finally, one might wonder whether the apparently problematic cases could be addressed by dissociating explanatory priority from ontological priority in

---

[38] These are Ammonius (*In cat.* 76.10–30), Elias (*In cat.* 213.17–215.17), Olympiodorus (*In cat.* 108.4–110.5), Philoponus (*In cat.* 117.15–124.14), Sergius of Rešᶜainā (*Introduction* §§75–79; *Categories* §§334–342), Simplicius (*In Cat.* 189.19–196.33), and the anonymous paraphrast (*Cat. par.* 35.14–36.34). See also al-Fārābī (*Cat. par.* §25) and Averroes (*Categories* §§58–59).

[39] I will address in the next section a recent argument (Mesquita, 2025) that, while Aristotle should not, by his own lights, and for the reasons mentioned by the commentators, endorse non-simultaneous correlatives, he endorses them for bad reasons in *Categories* 7 and corrects this mistake in *Metaphysics* 5.

the way that I discussed earlier (p. 18) as a strategy that some attempt for interpreting *Cat.* 12. In addition to the controversial commitments of that strategy that I mentioned previously, the strategy cannot account for the full range of apparently problematic cases. In order for it to do so, it would need to be true that in each such case the mutual dependence between x and y is explanatory but not ontological and the priority of x to y is ontological but not explanatory, or the mutual dependence between x and y is ontological but not explanatory and the priority of x to y is explanatory but not ontological. In short, in each of the apparently problematic cases the direction of ontological dependence and the direction of explanatory dependence would need to be different. But this is not so. Consider perceptible and perception, for example. The perceptible is ontologically prior to perception. But since Aristotle has a causal theory of perception, he thinks that the perceptible is also explanatorily prior to perception. Ontological and explanatory dependence run in the same direction in this case.[40]

Aristotle, then, appears to have a very serious problem. Numerous cases that he says are examples of ontological priority apparently cannot be such examples. That is because if these are examples of ontological priority then, apparently, it will be true both that one of a pair of things can be without the other and that it cannot be without the other. These cases cannot be dismissed as peripheral, for they are central to his theory of causation, mathematics, hylomorphism, and psychology.

4 Aristotle's Answer to the Priority Problem

I will now argue that Aristotle furnishes the resources to solve the Priority Problem. I will end by clarifying how, and in light of what commitments, this Aristotelian answer to the Priority Problem can be adapted to address the most compelling challenges to grounding's intuitive status as inducing a strict partial order on its domain.

4.1 Diagnosing a Fallacy

One of the fallacies that Aristotle discusses in *Sophistical Refutations* is what comes to be known as the *fallacia secundum quid et simpliciter*, or *secundum quid* for short (*SE* 5, 166^{b}37–167^{a}20 and 25, 180^{a}23–^{b}40). Fallacious inferences of this type can run in two directions, namely from a thing under some qualification (*secundum quid*) to the thing unqualified (*simpliciter*) or vice versa:

---

[40] Thanks to Riin Sirkel for prompting discussion of this point.

Secundum quid ad simpliciter If a is F *qua* G, then a is F.
Simpliciter ad secundum quid If a is F, then a is F *qua* G.

Here is how Aristotle describes this type of fallacy:

Fallacies that depend on what is said unqualifiedly, or instead in some respect and not strictly, arise when what is said in a particular way is taken as if said unqualifiedly.

Οἱ δὲ παρὰ τὸ ἁπλῶς τόδε ἢ πῇ λέγεσθαι καὶ μὴ κυρίως, ὅταν τὸ ἐν μέρει λεγόμενον ὡς ἁπλῶς εἰρημένον ληφθῇ

SE 5, 166ᵇ37–167ᵃ1

Arguments that depend on what is said to be this strictly speaking, or in some respect, place, manner, or relation, rather than without qualification, should be resolved by investigating the conclusion with reference to its contradictory to assess whether one of these may have occurred. For contraries and opposites, or an affirmation and denial, cannot belong to the same thing without qualification, though nothing prevents each from belonging in some respect, relation, or manner, or one belonging in some respect and the other without qualification. So, if one belongs without qualification and the other in some respect, there is as yet no refutation, but this should be examined in the conclusion with reference to its contradictory.

Τοὺς δὲ παρὰ τὸ κυρίως τόδε ἢ πῇ ἢ ποὺ ἢ πῶς ἢ πρός τι λέγεσθαι, καὶ μὴ ἁπλῶς, λυτέον σκοποῦντι τὸ συμπέρασμα πρὸς τὴν ἀντίφασιν, εἰ ἐνδέχεται τούτων τι πεπονθέναι. τὰ γὰρ ἐναντία καὶ τὰ ἀντικείμενα καὶ φάσιν καὶ ἀπόφασιν ἁπλῶς μὲν ἀδύνατον ὑπάρχειν τῷ αὐτῷ, πῇ μέντοι ἑκάτερον ἢ πρός τι ἢ πῶς, ἢ τὸ μὲν πῇ τὸ δ' ἁπλῶς, οὐδὲν κωλύει. ὥστ' εἰ τόδε μὲν ἁπλῶς τόδε δὲ πῇ, οὔπω ἔλεγχος, τοῦτο δ' ἐν τῷ συμπεράσματι θεωρητέον πρὸς τὴν ἀντίφασιν.

SE 25, 180ᵃ23–31

This fallacy has a range of subtypes, some of which are distinguished by Boethius and later commentators, but the basic idea is that in contexts sensitive to qualification of the subject in a particular way, ignoring the qualification disrupts the inference. Two such contexts about which Aristotle says a great deal elsewhere are those of specifying correlatives and specifying cause and effect. Such proper specification is what rules out explanation-thwarting accidentality. Consider correlatives first. Aristotle thinks that there are different possible qualifications of entities, under some of which the entities are genuine correlatives and under others of which they are not. For example, while two individuals qualified as members of the human species, or as bipeds or as musical, are not correlatives, they are when qualified as master and slave (*Cat.* 7, 7ᵃ28–30). The subjects qualified in the latter way, that is to say, properly specified, are "*per se* correlatives," and the subjects qualified in some other way, or considered simply as subjects of qualification, are "accidental correlatives" (*Cat.* 7, 7[a]25–28; *Top.* 6.4, 142[a]26–31, 6.8, 146[a]36–[b]6; *Metaph.* 5.15, 1021[b]3–11).

Just as there are *per se* and accidental correlatives, there are *per se* and accidental causes and effects. Polycleitus *qua* actively sculpting and the sculpture *qua* actively being sculpted are related as actual *per se* cause and effect (*Phys.* 2.3, 195[a]27–[b]12), whereas Polycleitus and the bronze are not. Polycleitus qualified in any way other than as sculpting (for example, as a human being or pale or musical) would be an accidental cause rather than a *per se* cause of the sculpture, and in any way other than as actually sculpting would be at best a potential *per se* cause. Likewise, Polycleitus qualified in any way other than as actually sculpting would not be *per se* correlative to the sculpture. This situation obtains for actual *per se* causes and effects in general (*Metaph.* 5.15, 1021[a]14–29).[41]

On Aristotle's view, Polycleitus is a subject who can be qualified by the predicate 'sculpting.' The resulting qualification, Polycleitus *qua* sculpting, differs in account from Polycleitus. This is because, for example, they have a different temporal scope of existence, and whereas Polycleitus survives a cessation of active sculpting, Polycleitus *qua* sculpting does not (*Phys.* 1.7, 190[a]13–21). Aristotle regards the qualification, Polycleitus *qua* sculpting (not only the property, *sculpting*), as accidental to Polycleitus (*Phys.* 2.3, 195[a]34–35). Polycleitus, the subject, is ontologically prior to this and other qualifications accidental to him.[42] The same goes for the bronze: It is ontologically prior to the bronze *qua* being sculpted. Polycleitus *qua* sculpting this bronze now and the bronze *qua* being sculpted by Polycleitus now, though, are correlatives. Neither can be without the other. Polycleitus is ontologically prior to the bronze *qua* being sculpted by him now since he can be without it, but it cannot be without him. These relationships can be visualized in Figure 2.

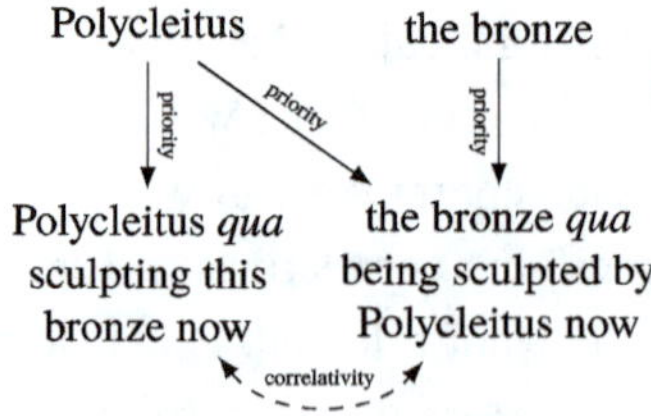

Figure 2 Ontological priority with correlativity.

---

[41] See Stein (2012, 870 n. 31) for comments on correlatives and *per se* efficient causation and Reece (2019, pp. 217–218) for comments on qualification of *per se* efficient causes.

[42] See, e.g., *Metaph.* 7.1, 1028[a]24–31 and remarks about it by Cohen (2008, p. 16) and Peramatzis (2011, p. 232). Lederman (2014) discusses the more general class of "coupled entities," only some of which are accidental unities, and their ontological posteriority to their underliers.

The distinction between a subject (e.g., Polycleitus) and a qualification of that subject (e.g., Polycleitus *qua* actively sculpting) can be used to solve the Priority Problem for Aristotle. There can seem to be cases in which Aristotle says that x is both ontologically prior to and correlative with y only if a distinction between a subject and a qualification of that subject is not observed. To see this, consider why, for Aristotle, the following would not be a case of reflexive priority: Polycleitus is prior to Polycleitus sculpting (*Phys.* 1.6, 189ª31–32), but if Polycleitus sculpting *is* Polycleitus then Polycleitus will be ontologically prior to himself. When we observe the distinction between a subject and a qualification of it, we can see that Polycleitus sculpting is Polycleitus only in the sense of being a qualification of the subject Polycleitus (*Phys.* 2.3, 195ª34–35). As Aristotle makes clear, this sort of 'is,' like any 'is' that does not entail sameness in account (*logos*), does not permit intersubstitution (*SE* 24, 179ª35–39; *Phys.* 3.3, 202ᵇ14–16). It is precisely because of a failure to recognize that a subject and a qualification of that subject are relevantly distinct, and therefore not intersubstitutable, that one would become confused about the ontological priority of a subject to qualifications of it (*Metaph.* 4.2, 1004ᵇ1–10).[43]

We are now equipped to return to the issue of whether Aristotle endorses non-simultaneous correlatives. I indicated earlier (p. 27 n. 39) that I would address the claim of António Pedro Mesquita (2025) that Aristotle in *Categories* 7 mistakenly commits to non-simultaneous correlatives, uses bad arguments to do so, and corrects this mistake in *Metaphysics* 5. Notwithstanding Mesquita's thorough study of this difficult section of *Categories*, I side with most commentators: I see nothing in *Categories* that forces the conclusion that Aristotle "overlooks or disregards" (Mesquita, 2025, p. 64) the distinction that would solve the problem of showing how he could believe that all correlatives reciprocate and offer apparent examples of non-simultaneous correlatives. The distinction that Mesquita thinks would solve the problem, the distinction that he thinks the ancient commentators on *Categories* think solves the problem, and the distinction that he thinks Aristotle thinks in *Metaphysics* 5 solves the problem, are the same distinction. This distinction is a specific version of the distinction that Aristotle repeatedly urges in the immediately preceding lines (*Cat.* 7, 6ᵇ36–7ᵇ14): *per se* correlatives require correct specification, whereas incorrect specification yields accidental correlatives.

---

[43] The rudiments of this solution to the Priority Problem can be found in the answer given to the question of whether Aristotle in fact endorses non-simultaneous correlatives by Ammonius (*In cat.* 76.10–30), Olympiodorus (*In cat.* 109.13–19), Philoponus (*In cat.* 122.25–123.10), and especially Sergius of Rešᶜainā (*Introduction* §§75–79; *Categories* §§334–342). These say that adequately specified correlatives are in every case simultaneous, though for some correlative pairs one of the things (*pragmata*) in its own right is prior to the other.

Aristotle's insistence upon correct specification of correlatives is in its turn a specific application of his recognition in *Sophistical Refutations* of how to avoid the *fallacia secundum quid et simpliciter*. I find it difficult to suppose that Aristotle suddenly and temporarily loses sight of the applicability of a point that he has made in the preceding lines. But, says Mesquita (2025, p. 39), Aristotle offers *arguments* that there are non-simultaneous correlatives (which arguments, Mesquita adds, are demonstrably unsound by Aristotle's own lights because of the very distinction under discussion). I reply that Aristotle indeed does so, but there is no need to interpret these as arguments the conclusion (or premises) of which Aristotle endorses in unqualified form. Rather, they can be viewed as reasons why it "would seem" to some people, namely those who do not heed Aristotle's repeated warnings about correct specification of correlatives, that some correlatives are non-simultaneous. This way of understanding the status of these arguments is reinforced by the way in which Aristotle concludes the chapter, namely by indicating that he has presented a series of puzzles (*Cat.* 7, 8^{b}23–24). The fact that Aristotle refrains from explicitly solving these puzzles before moving on to another topic does not force us to conclude that he has forgotten or failed to notice the applicability of the distinction that he draws earlier in the chapter. We are left with little reason to suppose that he here (suddenly, temporarily, and by his own lights mistakenly) endorses non-simultaneous correlatives.

I now return to the distinction between a subject and a qualification of that subject that is needed for solving the Priority Problem. Multiple ways of spelling out how these can be relevantly distinct are available within the formal limits of the solution that I advocate to the Priority Problem:[44] A constraint on admissible ways of spelling it out is that they do not universally validate *secundum quid et simpliciter* inferences.[45]

Conceptual distinction Introduced entirely by our way of cognizing or describing, e.g., Polycleitus vs. Polycleitus cognized/described as sculpting[46]

---

[44] Thanks to James Van Cleve for discussion of this issue. For extensive historical background on accounts of qualification see Bäck (1996). Note that though Aristotle uses '*qua*' in *Cat.* 7, he does not explain whether or how to situate it within his categorial scheme. Thanks to an anonymous reviewer for suggesting clarification about this.

[45] Loets (2021, p. 19), referring to a principle that she calls "Collapse," – though she does not say so, Collapse simply asserts the universal validity of *secundum quid ad simpliciter* inferences – argues that "Collapse cannot hold on any admissible theory of qualification."

[46] Ackrill (1981, p. 38), Kirwan (1971, p. 181), Lear (1982, pp. 168–169), Meister (2020), Miller (1973, p. 484), Moravcsik (1975, p. 633), Sorabji (1980, p. 4), and Williams (1985, p. 68) speak of Aristotle's distinction as if it is conceptual. Fine's (1982, p. 103) claim that *qua*-objects "are not genuinely 'out there' in the world, but are formed from what is out there by means of an

Realis major distinction Worldly numerical distinctness, e.g., Polycleitus vs. the mereological sum of Polycleitus and sculpting[47]

Realis minor distinction Intermediate between conceptual and *realis major* distinctions: compatible with numerical sameness but featuring a distinction with a worldly basis, such as one in form, mode, *vel sim.*, e.g., Polycleitus vs. a mode/formality of Polycleitus[48]

Pluralism The distinction between a subject and a qualification of that subject can be construed in more than one of these ways depending on the case at issue.[49]

How one thinks that intersubstitution of a subject and a qualification of it is blocked varies in accordance with which one of these four approaches one takes. Proponents of the *realis major* distinction (major realists) can say that Polycleitus and Polycleitus *qua* sculpting are numerically distinct, though accidentally the same, on the grounds that accidental sameness (coincidental compresence) is not numerical identity. They can then add that a relation is reflexive if and only if it permits intersubstitution of numerical identicals, but since x and x *qua* F are accidentally the same and not numerically identical, they are not intersubstitutable. Those who prefer the conceptual or *realis minor* distinctions (conceptualists, minor realists) can say that there are two types of sameness in number, accidental sameness and intrinsic sameness (*Metaph.* 5.9, $1017^{b}27$–$1018^{a}9$), and while some contexts might permit intersubstitution of x and y where these are accidentally the same, other contexts, including priority/grounding contexts, will not. For conceptualists, whether a context is such as to permit intersubstitution of x and y, where these are accidentally the same, is descriptively sensitive, so description/conceptualization introduces variability in the context that determines what kind(s) of numerical sameness would

---

alliance with a purely intensional element" is perhaps suggestive of a conceptual distinction. Szabó's (2003) account of qualifiers as adjunct predicates requires no more than a conceptual distinction.

[47] Charles (1984, pp. 27–29, 251–255) and Charles (2021, 46 n.9), Cohen (2008), F. A. Lewis (1982), Matthews (1982), and Peramatzis (2011, pp. 170–171) suppose that Aristotle's distinction is a *realis major*. Yablo's (1987) account of coincidence is one way of articulating a *realis major* distinction.

[48] Dancy (1975, pp. 361–368) and Spellman (1995, pp. 28–31) contend that Aristotle's distinction is a *realis minor*. John Duns Scotus gives the most famous version of the *realis minor*, his formal distinction, explained, e.g., at *Reportata Parisiensia* t. I, d. 33, qq. 2–3 and d. 34 q. 1. (For an especially helpful recent treatment of Scotus's various distinctions, including the formal distinction, see Blander, 2020.) Francisco Suárez has a modal distinction (*DM* 7.1). Baxter (2018) offers a current account of the distinction between subjects and qualifications as a *realis minor*.

[49] Hennig (2024, p. 202), though he draws a different set of distinctions between accounts of qualification, tentatively suggests that "It might actually be better to have a range of specific and limited accounts, each of which targets only a limited number of cases."

permit intersubstitution in that context, and therefore what sort of numerical sameness is at issue for irreflexivity in that context. For minor realists, any context that is sensitive to differences in essence, formality, kind membership, or mode (depending on the version of *realis minor* distinction adopted) will be such that intersubstitution will fail for x and y where these are accidentally, but not intrinsically, the same. Conceptualism offers the weakest distinction between subjects and qualifications of them but requires the least obvious way of blocking their intersubstitutivity. By contrast, major realism requires the strongest distinction but has the easiest way of blocking intersubstitutivity. Minor realism is intermediate in both respects. According to pluralism intersubstitution can fail for different reasons depending on the case under consideration.

4.2 Examples Revisited

Consider now the cases that motivated the Priority Problem. These seemed to be instances in which x is prior to, but also correlative with, y. However, once we recognize the importance of distinguishing between a subject and a qualification of it, we can see that the structure of the examples is more complicated: in each case, some x is ontologically prior to some y and to some qualification, r, of y, and some qualification, q, of x is *per se* correlative with r. But since x is distinct in account from q, x is only accidentally correlative with r. No two things that are the same in account are such that one of them is both ontologically prior to, and correlative with, the other. So, the apparently problematic cases are merely apparently problematic.

Distinguishing between subjects and qualifications of them deals with the aforementioned cases as follows. The qualifications of these entities that I list here are not meant to reflect every nuance of Aristotle's intricate discussions of knowledge, thought, perception, causation, hylomorphism, and mathematics. Rather, I intend to say enough only to inspire confidence that, in a fully worked-out description, the qualifications that are *per se* correlatives would differ in account from the subjects that are such that one is ontologically prior to the other. I use '⋈' to itemize correlative pairs and '<' to itemize ordered pairs in which the first item is ontologically prior to the second.

- knowable, knowledge
  - ⋈ knowable *qua* demonstratively grasped, knowledge *qua* demonstrative grasp
  - < mind-independent fact/object signified by a necessarily true proposition, knowledge *qua* demonstrative grasp of it

- perceptible, perception
  - ⋈ perceptible *qua* actively producing apprehension of the form without the matter, perception *qua* active process of apprehending the form without the matter
  - < underlying subject bearing a certain form, perception *qua* active process of apprehending that form
- thinkable, thought
  - ⋈ thinkable *qua* intuitively grasped, thought *qua* intuitive grasp
  - < mind-independent fact/object signified by a necessarily true proposition, thought *qua* intuitive grasp of it
- what acts upon something, that upon which it acts
  - ⋈ what acts *qua* actual *per se* cause, that upon which it acts *qua* actual *per se* effect
  - < bearer of a certain form, what is acted upon *qua* material subject apt to receive that form
- the form of a natural object, its matter
  - ⋈ form *qua* enforming this matter, matter *qua* enformed by this form
  - < form *qua* actuality/essence, matter *qua* potentiality
- monad, dyad
  - ⋈ monad *qua* half, dyad *qua* double
  - < monad, dyad
- circle, semicircle
  - ⋈ semicircle *qua* half, circle *qua* double
  - < circle, semicircle

The proposed way of addressing these cases explains both why it succeeds in handling those cases and why it would similarly handle any such cases: only *per se* correlatives, not accidental correlatives, are mutually ontologically dependent. That is because only items that reciprocate are mutually ontologically dependent and accidental correlatives do not reciprocate (*Cat.* 7, 7ª25–30). But in the case of some accidental correlatives, namely those accidental correlatives for which one can be without the other but not vice versa, one can be ontologically prior to another. But it is impossible for any entities to be *per se* correlatives and accidental correlatives under the same qualification. This explains not only *that* but also *why* it is impossible for any x to be ontologically prior to, and yet mutually dependent on, some y where x and y are the same in account.

If what I have just said is correct, then dependence of x on y does not entail that y is ontologically prior to x. After all, *per se* correlatives are mutually ontologically dependent, but neither is ontologically prior to the other. This and analogous non-entailments are interesting in their own right,[50] but it is worth noticing that the non-entailment is evidentially downstream of the more specific position that I have attributed to Aristotle. In other words, his rejection of the entailment is revealed by the remarks that support the specific position that I have attributed to him. Since Aristotle's apparent problem arises from within the perspective of his own theory, as determined by the set of available textual evidence for what his theory is, that problem must be shown to be merely apparent from the same perspective, as determined by the set of available textual evidence. His solution to his problem must be understood to correspond to the level of specificity at which the evidence actually occurs. This evidence supports attributing to Aristotle a specific position that is a determinate way of denying the entailment: It is precisely by drawing attention to the dependence of *per se* correlatives on subjects and on each other that he distinguishes them from subjects, which are apt to be described as ontologically prior to those things that depend upon them. In other words, a subject is the sort of thing that is expected to be ontologically prior to that which ontologically depends on it. No such expectation attaches to qualifications of subjects. (One might treat a qualification of a subject as, in turn, a subject* for a more complex qualification, but then this subject* could not be *per se* correlative to the more complex qualification if, as Aristotle apparently thinks, *per se* correlativity requires a commensurate degree of complexity of the correlatives.) There are, then, differences in what we can infer from dependence that track differences in whether x is a subject or a qualification of a subject. Aristotle's way of appealing to the distinction between subjects and qualifications of them, and not only the mere fact that the dependence of x on y does not entail the priority of y to x, is the available evidence that he can address the cases that motivated the Priority Problem.

---

[50] I have already mentioned Barnes (2018) and Bolzano (*Wissenschaftslehre* vol. 2, part 3, §202 and §209), who deny that dependence and determination, respectively, entail grounding. Barnes gives the following examples of symmetrical dependence that she thinks are not examples of grounding: universals corresponding to natural kinds depend on their instances and vice versa, states of affairs and their constituents depend on each other, mass tropes, size tropes, shape tropes, etc. depend on each other, positions in a mathematical structure depend on each other, and the event of World War II and the event of the evacuation of Dunkirk depend on each other. Bolzano gives these examples of determination without grounding: the equation $2x = b$ determines, but does not ground, the quantity x, indicating a body's position determines, but does not ground, its being, and the sides and angles of a triangle determine, but do not ground, each other.

4.3 Textual Evidence for Application of the Proposed Solution

Aristotle's diagnosis of the *fallacia secundum quid et simpliciter* in *Sophistical Refutations* 25 shows us that he recognizes the general importance of distinguishing between a subject and a qualification of it. But there is also substantial textual evidence that he views this distinction as useful for solving the Priority Problem. In some texts, he holds that some *x* is ontologically prior to some *y* and to some qualification of *y*, and that some qualification of *x* and some qualification of *y* are *per se* correlatives. For example, he thinks that biological substances are ontologically prior to their organs and denies that they are correlatives (*Cat.* 7, 8ᵇ21) but says that certain qualifications of such substances are correlative to certain qualifications of their organs. A bird is ontologically prior to its wing, but certain qualifications of the bird and its wing are *per se* correlatives. As Aristotle puts it, "the wing is a wing of a winged thing and the winged thing is a winged thing with a wing" (*Cat.* 7, 7ᵃ4–5). He views such awkwardness in expression as necessary to give a fully accurate description of the qualifications that are *per se* correlatives, and he understands that descriptions that are less accurate from the point of view of specifying correlatives will yield accidental correlatives.

Additional evidence can be found in some of his remarks about perception, particularly those in which he articulates what is wrong with the conventionalist antirealism of Democritus, Protagoras, and others who think that there is no perceptible without perception. Let us begin with this:

In general, if only the perceptible is, nothing would be unless animate things are, since perception would not be. So, while on the one hand it is presumably true that neither perceptibles nor perceptions would be (for perception is an affection of the perceiver), on the other it is impossible for the underlying subjects that produce perception not to be, even without perception being. That is because perception is surely not of itself, but rather there is some distinct thing beyond the perception which, necessarily, is prior to the perception. For, the mover is prior in nature to the moved, and even if these are correlative to each other this is no less true.

ὅλως τ᾽ εἴπερ ἔστι τὸ αἰσθητὸν ᵇ30
μόνον, οὐθὲν ἂν εἴη μὴ ὄντων τῶν
ἐμψύχων· αἴσθησις γὰρ οὐκ ἂν
εἴη. τὸ μὲν οὖν μήτε τὰ αἰσθητὰ
εἶναι μήτε τὰ αἰσθήματα ἴσως ἀλη-
θές (τοῦ γὰρ αἰσθανομένου πάθος
τοῦτό ἐστι), τὸ δὲ τὰ ὑποκείμε-
να μὴ εἶναι, ἃ ποιεῖ τὴν αἴσθησιν,
καὶ ἄνευ αἰσθήσεως, ἀδύνατον. οὐ ᵇ35
γὰρ δὴ ἥ γ᾽ αἴσθησις αὐτὴ ἑαυτῆς
ἐστίν, ἀλλ᾽ ἔστι τι καὶ ἕτερον παρὰ
τὴν αἴσθησιν, ὃ ἀνάγκη πρότερον
εἶναι τῆς αἰσθήσεως· τὸ γὰρ κινοῦν
τοῦ κινουμένου φύσει πρότερόν ἐ-
στι, κἂν εἰ λέγεται πρὸς ἄλληλα ᵃ1
ταῦτα, οὐθὲν ἧττον.

Metaph. 4.5, 1010ᵇ30–1011ᵃ2

In this passage, Aristotle indicates that perceptible and perception, as species of mover and moved, respectively, are correlatives, and so neither could be without the other. At least part of the reason that he gives for thinking this is that perception is an affection of the perceiver. But perception qualified as the ability to apprehend the form without the matter is not an affection of the perceiver; only perception qualified as the active process of apprehending the form without the matter is. Likewise, the underlying subject, which may be referred to as "the perceptible" because it happens to be capable of producing perception in virtue of bearing the form that perception will in fact apprehend, has nothing intrinsically to do with the perceiver; only the underlying subject qualified as actively producing apprehension of the form without the matter, which production is realized in the perceiver, does. Nevertheless, the underlying subject bearing a certain form is ontologically prior to perception qualified as the active process of apprehending that form without the matter since the underlying subject can be without perception thus qualified, but not vice versa. So, under one qualification the perceptible and perception are correlatives, and the underlying subject that happens to be perceived is ontologically prior to perception. Some of these details emerge even more clearly in the following:

Since the actuality of the perceptible and of what is capable of perceiving are one, though their being is different, it is necessary that what are spoken of as 'hearing' and 'sounding' in this way (viz., as active) are destroyed or preserved together, and likewise for flavor and tasting and the other cases. But it is not necessary for those spoken of as potential. The earlier natural philosophers did not speak well about this, since they thought that neither white nor black is apart from sight, nor flavor apart from taste. In one way they spoke correctly, in another incorrectly. That is because 'perception' and 'perceptible' are said in two ways, namely, as potential and as active, and what was said by them applies in the latter case but not in the former. They spoke unqualifiedly about things that are not said unqualifiedly.

ἐπεὶ δὲ μία μέν ἐστιν ἐνέργεια ἡ 15
τοῦ αἰσθητοῦ καὶ τοῦ αἰσθητικοῦ,
τὸ δ' εἶναι ἕτερον, ἀνάγκη ἅμα
φθείρεσθαι καὶ σώζεσθαι τὴν οὕτω
λεγομένην ἀκοὴν καὶ ψόφον, καὶ
χυμὸν δὴ καὶ γεῦσιν, καὶ τὰ
ἄλλα ὁμοίως· τὰ δὲ κατὰ δύναμιν
λεγόμενα οὐκ ἀνάγκη· ἀλλ' οἱ
πρότερον φυσιολόγοι τοῦτο οὐ 20
καλῶς ἔλεγον, οὐθὲν οἰόμενοι οὔτε
λευκὸν οὔτε μέλαν εἶναι ἄνευ
ὄψεως, οὐδὲ χυμὸν ἄνευ γεύσεως.
τῇ μὲν γὰρ ἔλεγον ὀρθῶς, τῇ δ'
οὐκ ὀρθῶς· διχῶς γὰρ λεγομένης
τῆς αἰσθήσεως καὶ τοῦ αἰσθητοῦ,
τῶν μὲν κατὰ δύναμιν τῶν δὲ
κατ' ἐνέργειαν, ἐπὶ τούτων μὲν
συμβαίνει τὸ λεχθέν, ἐπὶ δὲ τῶν 25
ἑτέρων οὐ συμβαίνει. ἀλλ' ἐκεῖνοι
ἁπλῶς ἔλεγον περὶ τῶν λεγομένων
οὐχ ἁπλῶς.

DA 3.2, 426ᵃ15–26

Aristotle is here more explicit: Only the perceptible qualified as active and perception qualified as active are correlatives (being "destroyed or preserved together," which language Aristotle uses to describe correlatives in *Cat.* 7). This does not hold of the perceptible qualified as potential and perception qualified as potential.[51] Democritus, Protagoras, and other conventionalist antirealists failed to give a proper account precisely because they spoke about the perceptible and perception without qualification instead of isolating, as Aristotle does, the qualification under which each counts as correlative to the other. Their accounts failed in denying without qualification that the perceptible can be without perception but not vice versa, or in other words, in denying without qualification that the perceptible (the underlying subject bearing a certain form that happens to be perceived) is ontologically prior to perception. Aristotle, by distinguishing between underlying subjects and qualifications of them, is able to give an account according to which perceptible and perception under some qualifications are correlatives even though the underlying subject bearing a certain form that happens to be perceived is ontologically prior to perception.

5 An Aristotelian Vindication of Grounding as Inducing a Strict Partial Order

Aristotle's answer to the Priority Problem puts us in view of a unified, principled way of addressing the most compelling purported counterexamples to the asymmetry, irreflexivity, and transitivity of grounding. I will discuss these in the order in which I mentioned them earlier.

5.1 Asymmetry

In Thompson's (2016b, 2018) alleged example of symmetrical grounding, a circle and the semicircles that it comprises are mutually ontologically dependent: The circle would not be without them and they would not be without it. Likewise, according to her, an organism and its organs are mutually ontologically dependent. However, if we, wishing to avoid committing the *fallacia secundum quid et simpliciter* that Aristotle discusses in *Sophistical Refutations* 5 and 25, follow him in distinguishing subjects from qualifications of those subjects, we arrive at a plausible diagnosis of Thompson's examples. The circle in its own right grounds the semicircles *qua* potential results of dividing it, but it is *qua* double and half that they are mutually ontologically dependent.

---

[51] Aristotle also indicates that qualifying the relevant items as potential or actual is important for parts and wholes (*Metaph.* 5.11, 1019^{a}7–10). He mentions the half-line and the whole, but the point also applies to the semicircle and the circle.

Likewise, an organism grounds its organs *qua* instruments functioning to support its life activities, but these are mutually dependent when qualified as a whole composed of organic parts and organic parts of a whole, respectively. In both examples, the grounding claim is true under one qualification and the mutual dependence claim is true under a different qualification. So, these are not genuine examples of symmetrical grounding.

I have presented an alternative to Thompson's diagnosis of her examples, but one might still wonder why my diagnosis is preferable. The reasons are as follows. First, Thompson (2018, p. 111) argues as if dependence entails grounding (see also 2018, p. 107):

> Take, for example, the grounding between facts about an organism and its [*sic*] facts about its organs. It seems, for example, that the fact that the heart pumps blood around the body depends on the fact that the organism exists and has a properly functioning circulatory system. But the fact that the organism exists and has a properly functioning circulatory system depends on the fact that the heart pumps blood around the body.

There are reasons to deny that dependence entails grounding, as I mentioned previously, so it is better to avoid commitment to that entailment if possible.[52]

Second, Thompson's argument for why we should understand her examples as instances of symmetrical grounding commits her to the symmetry of explanation: The reason for thinking that the circle and semicircles ground each other is that they explain each other's existence (2018, p. 111). But most who comment on the relationship between grounding and explanation think that explanation is asymmetric, as I mentioned earlier (p. 4 n. 9).

5.2 Irreflexivity

Jenkins's (2011) alleged example of reflexive grounding, where a subject's brain state and the pain that, on her view, is identical with that brain state ground each other, can be answered similarly, though the exact details of what the relevant subject(s) and qualification(s) are will depend on one's theory of the mind. If we take it that the underlying subject is the brain state and pain is the brain state *qua* phenomenal presentation of a certain kind, then it will be true to say that both are the same in some sense, but the subject (the brain state) grounds the qualification of it (brain state *qua* phenomenal presentation of a certain kind).

---

[52] Bolzano (*Wissenschaftslehre* vol. 2, part 3, §209) discusses a merely apparent counterexample, due to Crusius, to the asymmetry of grounding that is similar in structure to Thompson's, namely one in which the sides and angles of a triangle are alleged to ground each other. Bolzano's diagnosis is that the example appears to be one of symmetrical grounding only if we think that if x determines (*bestimmt*) y then x grounds y, which he argues in §202 would be a mistake.

Or, if we think that there is one state that can be qualified either as a brain state or as a phenomenal presentation of a certain kind, the state *qua* brain state and the state *qua* phenomenal do not ground each other – rather, the state would ground each of the two qualifications – and neither qualification grounds itself. There are, of course, other possibilities, but whatever one's preferred theory of mind might be, Jenkins has given us no reason to think that there are any qualifications *q* and *r* of the state such that *q* and *r* ground each other or such that *q* grounds itself or *r* grounds itself. It is only by ignoring the distinction between subject and qualification that the example might seem to be one of reflexive grounding.

In the course of her discussion of the example that she says challenges the irreflexivity of grounding, Jenkins mentions that a hypothetical interlocutor might appeal (though she distances herself from such an appeal) to a certain type of *qua*-operator (not an Aristotelian *qua*-operator, as will be seen) in order to challenge the irreflexivity of grounding (as she does and I do not) while vindicating the "quasi-irreflexivity" of the *word* 'grounding.'[53] The place of Jenkins's hypothetical interlocutor's appeal within the dialectic of Jenkins's overall argument, the motivation for that appeal, and its content, reveal that it is merely superficially similar to, and indeed incompatible with, my Aristotelian proposal.

Although Jenkins does not commit to this appeal or to the alternatives to it that she discusses, and in fact expresses reservation about their premise that 'x metaphysically grounds itself' sounds bad (p. 268), her hypothetical interlocutor who makes the appeal to a certain sort of *qua*-operator is meant to do so in order to *challenge* grounding's irreflexivity, as Jenkins does. Basically, Jenkins and her hypothetical interlocutor both want to reject grounding's irreflexivity, but Jenkins feels less pressure than the interlocutor does to attempt to take the edge off of such a denial by honoring the linguistic intuition about "quasi-irreflexivity." Jenkins and her hypothetical interlocutor want to reject grounding's irreflexivity because, she says, it would entail that grounding

---

[53] Jenkins speaks of 'metaphysical dependence,' but treats it as synonymous with 'metaphysical grounding,' as she announces in n. 1. Thus Jenkins (2011, p. 268): "Convincing though it seems at first glance, I am not sure that the irreflexivity assumption is appropriate. Suppose I say that S's pain is metaphysically dependent upon some brain state. What happens if I then go on to *identify* the pain state with the brain state? Am I forced to go back and reject the dependence claim? The purpose of this paper is to investigate views on which I am not; views on which it might be acceptable to say things like: 'Of course S's pain depends on S's brain state. They are one and the same.' I will grant, for the sake of argument, that 'dependence' (the word, not the relation) is 'quasi-irreflexive'. By that I mean that it always sounds bad to say 'x metaphysically depends on x' or 'x metaphysically grounds itself'. This could, I think, be resisted; consideration of some of the cases considered in this paper might give rise to contexts where such utterances really don't sound bad at all. But let's pretend that it's established."

claims would require commitments about how to individuate objects that neither she nor the interlocutor wants to make. She gives the following example: "It's pretty plausible that statues depend metaphysically on the matter of which they are composed; but if that's true then the irreflexivity of dependence entails that no statue is identical to its matter" (p. 269). Jenkins and her hypothetical interlocutor reject grounding's irreflexivity in part because they want to be able, at least in principle, to affirm that a statue is identical to its matter.[54] Aristotelians about metaphysical structure, of course, are committed to rejecting the identity of a statue with its matter. So, there is already reason to believe that the appeal to the kind of *qua*-operator that Jenkins attributes to her hypothetical interlocutor cannot be the same kind of appeal that I have been discussing, since the motivation for the former sharply conflicts with a deep commitment associated with the latter.

The difference between the appeal made by Jenkins's hypothetical interlocutor and my Aristotelian proposal is also observable from the former's content. The interlocutor is meant to draw on David Lewis's (2003) counterpart-theoretic version of the *qua*-operator in order to *affirm* that the ground and grounded may be identical (that is, in order to deny that grounding is irreflexive) while explaining, rather than outright dismissing, the fact that grounding claims tend to be heard as directional.[55] The appearance of direction is due to the fact that in certain contexts different counterpart relations can be evoked for the same thing. A difference in counterpart relations is not an intrinsic difference, and so on Lewisian views does not imply non-identity, but it can make claims involving the thing whose counterpart relations are differently evoked sound different from each other. The Lewisian *qua*-operator permits precisely the problematic pattern of inference that Aristotle rejects in *Sophistical Refutations* 25, namely inferring that x or x *qua* F shares all intrinsic properties with x *qua* G. Deployment of Aristotle's *qua*-operator maintains the irreflexivity of grounding; deployment of the Lewisian version does not. Bennett (2017, p. 44) asserts that even if, contrary to fact, Lewisians wanted to *defend*

---

[54] This aspect of Jenkins's motivation might seem to invite general reflection, which I will not prioritize here, on the extent to which grounding's order-theoretic properties should be expected to foreclose options in first-order metaphysical debates. However, I think that the case that she mentions is more appropriately viewed as revealing a way in which attention to grounding's order-theoretic properties enables us to see why some ways of formulating first-order metaphysical claims would be confused, namely by their lacking order-theoretic coherence. Thanks to an anonymous reviewer for encouraging me to mention this point.

[55] Wilson (2014, p. 573) in fact makes such a Lewisian appeal in arguing that the identity relation is a kind of grounding relation but can be heard as directional. Guigon (2018, pp. 121–122) makes a similar Lewisian appeal, though without Wilson's claim about the identity relation itself.

irreflexivity by arguing that grounding claims introduce a context that does not permit intersubstitution of *x*, *x qua F*, and *x qua G*, their counterpart-theoretic semantics of the *qua*-operator would render them unable to offer any principled reason that grounding claims should introduce such a context when claims involving other comparative relations do not. I will return to Bennett's point in Section 5.5, p. 51.

5.3 Transitivity

5.3.1 Examples Revisited

Finally, consider Schaffer's (2012) challenge to the transitivity of grounding involving THE DENTED SPHERE, THE THIRD MEMBER, and THE CAT'S MEOW. Recall that each of these involves three claims, where the first features existential dependence of one thing on another, the second features a relationship of determinate to determinable or of a factual witness to an existential generalization, and the third, which Schaffer says would follow from the first two if grounding were transitive, does not feature the existential dependence that figures in the first, with the result that grounding is not transitive. Here again are the examples:

THE DENTED SPHERE Imagine a slightly imperfect sphere, with a minor dent.

⊜1 The fact that the thing has a dent grounds the fact that the thing has shape S

⊜2 The fact that the thing has shape S grounds the fact that it is more-or-less spherical

⊜3 The fact that the thing has a dent grounds the fact that it is more-or-less spherical

THE THIRD MEMBER Let S be a set with exactly three members, a, b, and c: $S = \{a, b, c\}$.

ᴬᴮc1 The fact that c is a member of S grounds the fact that S has exactly three members

ᴬᴮc2 The fact that S has exactly three members grounds the fact that S has finitely many members

ᴬᴮc3 The fact that c is a member of S grounds the fact that S has finitely many members

THE CAT'S MEOW Imagine that Cadmus the cat is meowing.

🐱1 The fact that the creature was produced from the meeting of this sperm and that ovum grounds the fact that Cadmus is meowing

🐱2 The fact that Cadmus is meowing grounds the fact that something is
   meowing

🐱3 The fact that the creature was produced from the meeting of this sperm
   and that ovum grounds the fact that something is meowing

For each of Schaffer's examples, I find myself at least as inclined to deny his first claim as to affirm his third. For each example, if the coarse-grained dependence in the first claim had been sufficient for grounding, so would that in the third claim.[56]

The foregoing discussion of Aristotle's account of ontological priority equips us with a diagnosis of this intuition. In particular, we have seen the importance of isolating the qualification under which something is *per se* explanatorily relevant to another. Otherwise, we risk the *fallacia secundum quid et simpliciter*. Each of Schaffer's examples can be read as featuring a qualification in at least one of the first two claims that calls *per se* explanatory relevance into question. In THE DENTED SPHERE, it is not *qua* having a dent that the thing has the shape that it does; rather, a more specific qualification is needed, such as being minorly dented and otherwise spherical,[57] or being dented in this particular way.[58] Under such qualifications, though, the corresponding fact would indeed ground the fact that this thing is more or less spherical and transitivity would not be violated. In other words, I think that in this case 'having a dent' is not a partial ground of the determinate shape, since a ground, whether full or partial, is *per se* explanatorily relevant to the grounded, but rather a

---

[56] Litland (2013, 21 n. 11) thinks that ⊖1 is false, that ^{ABC}3 is true if ^{ABC}2 is true (26), and that 🐱1 is false (29). Raven (2013, p. 199) thinks that ⊖3 is true and ^{ABC}1 and 🐱1 are false. Rodriguez-Pereyra (2015, pp. 521–522) thinks that ⊖1 and ^{ABC}1 are false.

[57] Raven (2013, p. 199): "Schaffer is right that a *different* dent would also suffice for *x*'s near-sphericality. But that doesn't preclude *this* dent from helping ground *x*'s near-sphericality. It does so with the help of other features of *x*. For example, in order for *x*'s having that dent to help ground its being nearly spherical, most of *x*'s surface points should be equidistant from its center point. Were most of *x*'s surface points not equidistant from its center point, then *x* wouldn't be nearly spherical, and so its having that dent wouldn't help to ground its near-sphericality. For example, were *x* nearly cubical, *x*'s having that dent would not help ground its near-sphericality (it's nearly cubical!) but would instead help ground its near-cubicality (together with different features of *x*). But given that most of *x*'s points are indeed equidistant from its center, the dent helps ground its near-sphericality."

[58] Litland (2013, 21 n. 11): "Schaffer uses 'has a dent' instead of 'has the particular dent it does'. But the grounding claim 'The fact that *a* has a dent grounds the fact that *a* has shape *S*' is surely false. What grounds *a*'s having shape *S* is not *a*'s having some-or-other dent – even one exactly like the one it in fact has – but rather its having the particular (type of) dent it has. We have to distinguish between claims of the forms '$(\exists x\phi) <$ ' and '$\exists x(\phi < \psi)$'. Alternatively put, when grounding is at issue we have to distinguish between the property of having a dent and the property of being dented."

partial *specification* of a partial ground, since the qualification under which *per se* relevance would obtain has not been given at the requisite level of specificity.[59]

In THE THIRD MEMBER, it is not in its own right that c being a member of S grounds S having exactly three members but rather *qua* member of S along with precisely two members distinct from c and from each other.[60] Since c *qua* member of S along with precisely two members distinct from c and from each other *does* ground S having finitely many members, transitivity does not fail. As in the previous example I think that Schaffer's formulation of his first premise adverts not to a partial ground but rather to a partial specification of a ground.

In THE CAT'S MEOW, it is not *qua* originated by a particular sperm and egg that Cadmus is meowing but rather *qua* vocalizing in this particular feline way (*vel sim.*).[61] But the fact that Cadmus is vocalizing in this particular feline way does ground the fact that something is meowing, so transitivity is not violated.[62]

Though my strategy for defending the transitivity of grounding overlaps with the remarks of Litland (2013), Raven (2013), and Rodriguez-Pereyra (2015), the fact that it is more unified and depends less on peculiarities of Schaffer's examples makes it more portable for responding to other candidate counter-examples. This is important for addressing a worry, expressed by Wilson (2014, p. 570) and endorsed by Bennett (2017, p. 38), that responding to apparent counterexamples is "increasingly ad hoc" as they become more numerous.

---

[59] Suppose, though, that we give a long, complicated, precise specification of the features of the dent, so that we achieve maximal clarity about being dented in this particular way. Will 🥣1 and 🥣2 then be true and 🥣3 false? I do not think so. If the long, complicated, precise specification of the dent's features is restricted to the dent, not amounting to a description of the solid with the dent, then I share Raven's intuition: 🥣1 does not ground 🥣2. But if the precise specification amounts to a description of the solid with the dent, then 🥣2 and 🥣3 follow from 🥣1. Thanks to Isaac Wilhelm for discussion of this.

[60] Rodriguez-Pereyra (2015, p. 522): "what grounds the fact that S has exactly three members is the fact that there is something, something else, and a third thing such that none of them is identical with either of the others, all three are members of S, and nothing else is."

[61] Litland (2013, p. 29): "What does the fact that Cadmus derived from this sperm and that ovum have to do with the fact that he is meowing? Whether he meows only turns on whether he is, well, meowing; it doesn't turn on how he originated. Facts about *what* something essentially is needn't be parts of the grounds for *how* that thing is."

[62] I leave aside the fact that the sort of appeal to existential generalization on which 🐱2 relies has been regarded as problematic. See, e.g., Fine (2010), Goodman (2023), Korbmacher (2018a, 2018b), and Wilhelm (2021)

5.3.2 Contrasts

At one level of description, my intuition is that each of Schaffer's examples features an explanatory disconnect because of an incomplete specification of the fact (or entity) in question. Schaffer shares the intuition at that level of description. He argues that grounding, as well as explanation, are *contrastive* relations, such that the relata are not individual facts (or entities) but rather differences between facts (or entities). Citing an individual fact (or entity) as ground and an individual fact (or entity) as grounded would then be insufficient. The specification would be incomplete because it would not include the contrast. Such an insufficiency shows us, says Schaffer, what went wrong in the three examples.

A more specific description of my intuition reveals how it differs from Schaffer's: Each of the examples features an explanatory disconnect because of a failure to isolate the appropriate qualification of the fact (or entity) in question. Such a failure is a way of being an incomplete specification. Here is why the difference between my proposal and Schaffer's matters: Schaffer thinks that his examples show that grounding does not exhibit transitivity but rather what he calls "differential transitivity." Differential transitivity applies to a proper subset of quaternary relations (in the simplest case) with contrastively specified relata (x rather than x^* stands in relation R to y rather than y^*), whereas transitivity applies to a proper subset of binary relations (in the simplest case).

Someone might prefer my proposal to the contrastivist strategy for dealing with the apparent counterexamples to the transitivity of grounding if one has certain intuitions about *why* grounding should exhibit non-monotonicity. This will require substantial explanation.[63] Informally, grounding is weakly non-monotonic if and only if the set of grounds of a grounded does not permit arbitrary expansion *salva veritate* and strongly non-monotonic if and only if the set of grounds of a grounded permits no expansion *salva veritate*. Formally, where '$\lhd$' represents the relational predicate 'grounds' and '$\ntriangleleft$' represents its negation:

Weak non-monotonicity $\neg \forall x, y, z(x \lhd y \rightarrow x \wedge z \lhd y)$
Strong non-monotonicity $\forall x, y, z(x \lhd y \rightarrow x \wedge z \ntriangleleft y)$

Repeating the example that I gave earlier of non-monotonicity, suppose that the constitution of Athens grounds Athens being a democracy. If grounding were monotonic, then we could safely infer that the constitution of Athens and the number of hairs in Solon's beard ground Athens being a democracy.

---

[63] I am grateful to Jonathan Schaffer and Isaac Wilhelm for discussion about this.

(For that matter, we could also safely infer that the constitution of Athens and Athens being a democracy grounds Athens being a democracy, thus violating the irreflexivity of grounding, as observed by Fine, 2012, p. 56 and deRosett, 2023, p. 35.) But this seems mistaken. Why? Many think that grounding is non-monotonic because every ground should exhibit (non-circular) relevance to the grounded or do work in making it the case.[64] The number of hairs of Solon's beard is irrelevant to Athens being a democracy and does no work in making it the case. Any example of this kind is enough to motivate weak non-monotonicity. According to strong non-monotonicity *any* expansion of the grounds in a true grounding claim will falsify it. The thought is basically that if something that did not appear on the list of grounds in a true grounding claim had been relevant for grounding the grounded, then it should have been mentioned in the true grounding claim.[65]

It is standardly held that grounding is at least weakly non-monotonic. Whether it is also strongly non-monotonic is more complicated. This is because there are apparent counterexamples to strong non-monotonicity if non-exclusive disjunctions are fully grounded by any of their disjuncts, conjunctions are partially grounded by any of their conjuncts, existential generalizations are fully grounded by any of their instances, or universal generalizations are partially grounded by any of their instances. Suppose, for example, that 'Fido is a dog or Felix is a cat' is grounded both by 'Fido is a dog' and by 'Felix is a cat.' We would then have a counterexample to strong non-monotonicity, for if 'Fido is a dog' grounds 'Fido is a dog or Felix is a cat' then so does 'Fido is a dog and Felix is a cat.' The same goes for 'Fido is a dog and Felix is a Cat.' This is likewise the case if the generalization that there are some pets is grounded both by a dog and by a cat, or if the generalization that every eighteenth-century president of the United States was a man is grounded both by Washington being a man and by Adams being a man. One might of course reply that construing disjunctive and existential grounding in this way is both unnecessary and problematic, for reasons discussed by, for example, Correia (2024, pp. 68–78), Fine (2010), Goodman (2023), Korbmacher (2018a, 2018b), Merlo (2022), and Wilhelm (2021). Rather, we might adopt weaker alternatives mentioned by Fine (2010, p. 108): "Any disjunctive truth is grounded by *a* disjunct" and "Any existential truth is grounded by *an* instance" (my emphasis). These weaker versions of disjunctive and existential grounding do not

---

[64] See Audi, (2012, p. 699; 2020, p. 571), Correia (2024, p. 11), Dasgupta (2014, p. 4), deRosett (2023, pp. 32–35), Fine (2012, p. 56), Guigon (2018, p. 117), Maurin (2019, p. 1581), Rosen (2010, pp. 116–117), Trogdon (2013, p. 109).

[65] Aristotle endorses an analogous claim about valid deductions in *APr* 1.1, 24^b18–21 and *Top.* 8.11, 161^b28–30, as noted by Malink (2022, 223 n. 10).

result in counterexamples to strong non-monotonicity of the aforementioned sort. No analogous reply is available in the case of conjunction and universal generalization, of course. This is unproblematic if strong non-monotonicity is meant to apply only to full grounding (not partial grounding), for conjuncts and instances are at most partial grounds of conjunctions and universal generalizations, respectively.[66] At any rate, one might plausibly insist that the statement of strong non-monotonicity was unnecessarily strong and that the core commitment about the relevance of ground to grounded that it encapsulates is one to which advocates of weak non-monotonicity should unhesitatingly agree:

Expansion intolerance $\forall x, y, z(x \lhd y \rightarrow (z \ntriangleleft y \rightarrow x \wedge z \ntriangleleft y))$
> Informally: Any true grounding claim is falsified by adding to the ground an item that does not ground the grounded.

Expansion intolerance captures the motivations for weak and strong non-monotonicity and permits none of the aforementioned kinds of counterexamples to the latter, whether for full or for partial grounding. A consequence of expansion intolerance is this:

Proliferation intolerance There are no distinct grounds of the same grounded where the distinction results from the introduction of items that do not ground the grounded. In other words, non-grounds never make the grounded ground-theoretically overdetermined.

With this picture of the motivations for, and implications of, a commitment to the non-monotonicity of grounding in view, let us now focus on contrastive grounding, which, since it can relate more than two terms (four in the simplest case), has two dimensions of expansion of grounds. In other words, there are two syntactically available mechanisms for adding to the ground. One is conjunction of differences: For example, the fact that the sphere is dented rather than being uniform can be conjoined with the fact that the sphere is dented rather than being yellow. Another is the addition of terms to a difference: For example, the fact that the sphere is dented rather than being uniform can be expanded to the fact that the sphere is dented rather than being uniform and rather than being yellow. This complication necessitates some delicacy in exploring the extent to which contrastive grounding accommodates a relevantly analogous version of expansion intolerance. In particular, it will be helpful to introduce a distinction between two kinds of differential expansion intolerance where these vary in accordance with the aforementioned distinction

---

[66] Audi (2012, p. 699) endorses strong non-monotonicity for full ground, and so evidently would Bolzano (*Wissenschaftslehre* vol. 2, part 3, §207), as noted by Roski (2020, p. 80).

between dimensions of expansion of grounds in a contrastive framework. In the following definitions, 'δ' expresses a relation that should be read as 'the difference between … on the one hand and … on the other,' ' … in contrast to … ,' ' … instead of … ,' or ' … rather than … ' The set X comprises obtaining facts, actually existing entities, and truths, whereas the set Y comprises non-obtaining facts, entities that do not actually exist, and falsehoods.

Wide differential expansion intolerance

$$\forall xy \in X, \forall x^*y^*z \in Y\left(\delta xx^* \vartriangleleft \delta yy^* \rightarrow \left((\delta xz \not\vartriangleleft \delta yy^*) \rightarrow (\delta xx^* \wedge \delta xz \not\vartriangleleft \delta yy^*)\right)\right)$$

> Informally: The conjunction of any difference that grounds a second difference with any difference that does not ground the second difference also does not ground the second difference.

Narrow differential expansion intolerance

$$\forall xy \in X, \forall x^*y^*z \in Y\left(\delta xx^* \vartriangleleft \delta yy^* \rightarrow \left((\delta xz \not\vartriangleleft \delta yy^*) \rightarrow (\delta xx^*z \not\vartriangleleft \delta yy^*)\right)\right)$$

> Informally: Any difference that grounds a second difference fails to ground it when its terms are supplemented by a non-obtaining term of a difference that does not ground the second difference.

Let us consider an example in order to appreciate the difference between wide and narrow differential expansion intolerance. Suppose that the fact that a sphere has a dent rather than having no dent grounds the fact that the sphere has shape S rather than having shape S*. Suppose, too, that the fact that the sphere has a dent rather than being yellow does not ground the fact that the sphere has shape S rather than having shape S*. The conjunction of the fact that the sphere has a dent rather than having no dent and the fact that the sphere has a dent rather than being yellow does not ground the fact that the sphere has shape S rather than having shape S*. So, wide differential expansion intolerance is not violated in this case. But narrow differential expansion intolerance is violated. That is because, from the perspective of contrastivism, the fact that the sphere has a dent rather than having no dent and rather than being yellow *does* ground the fact that the sphere has shape S rather than having shape S*. From the perspective of contrastivism, if the fact that the sphere has a dent rather than having no dent grounds the fact that the sphere has shape S rather than having shape S*, where having no dent is a non-obtaining fact, then adding further non-obtaining facts, such as that of being yellow, to the contrast should not affect the truth of the grounding claim. That is because in this case precisely one of the non-obtaining facts isolates the intended contrast with the obtaining fact. This requires some explanation. One important thing that this example reveals is that contrastive grounding permits an asymmetry between the obtaining term and each of the non-obtaining terms that does not apply between the non-obtaining terms: The non-obtaining terms isolate what it is about the obtaining term that is relevant. But one non-obtaining term does not isolate what it is about the other non-obtaining term that is relevant, or would be relevant, to the corresponding non-obtaining term in the grounded difference. Furthermore, at least in this example one of the non-obtaining terms is more important than the other is for delimiting the set of possible worlds to be considered in applying a counterfactual test, namely the one that restricts attention to the complement of the set of worlds delimited by the obtaining term. In other words, one non-obtaining term makes the bigger cut in the space of possible worlds to be considered for a counterfactual test. The other non-obtaining term(s) merely delimit(s) a proper subset of the complement of the set of worlds delimited by the obtaining term. This asymmetry between the obtaining term and each of the non-obtaining terms is some evidence that counterfactual tests for differential grounding claims are most appropriately applied to the *set* of non-obtaining terms rather than to each non-obtaining term serially. Furthermore, if they were not so applied then it would be difficult to see how adding a term to a difference is to be distinguished from conjoining quaternary differences, putting into doubt whether contrastivism is indeed generalizable, as Schaffer thinks it is, to differences of higher arity.

Though as we have just seen expansion by adding terms to a difference does not, on the contrastivist account, alter the relevance of that difference to the difference that it grounds or the work that it does in making that difference the case, it does result in a distinct difference if, as Schaffer (2009, p. 348; 2012, 134 n. 18) supposes, the terms are to be understood as "sets of contrasts." Since sets have their members essentially, adding a member (for example, another non-obtaining fact) results in a distinct set.

The previous two paragraphs can be summarized by noting that a slogan of Schaffer (2016, p. 74), "wiggle the ground, and the grounded wiggles," is revealed by the aforementioned counterexample to narrow differential expansion intolerance to be interestingly ambiguous: The slogan is true of the ground *qua* ground of the grounded, but false of the ground *qua* difference. It is because, from the contrastivist perspective, non-obtaining terms can affect the identity of a difference without affecting the difference's grounding of the grounded that this situation arises.

Recall the consequence of expansion intolerance mentioned on p. 48, namely proliferation intolerance. We are now in a position to see that contrastive grounding does not exhibit proliferation intolerance since it tolerates narrow differential expansion and adding a term to a difference results in a distinct difference. This means that contrastive grounding allows *arbitrarily many* distinct grounds of the same grounded where the distinction results from the introduction of items that are not involved in grounding the grounded. In other words, it allows that non-grounds *frequently* make the grounded ground-theoretically overdetermined. What is more, such overdetermination is not limited to the controversial kinds mentioned earlier, namely disjunction, conjunction, existential generalization, and universal generalization. The upshot is that contrastive grounding is at odds with a consequence of standard motivations for the non-monotonicity of grounding, unlike the account that I have offered.

5.4 The Unity of Grounding

While I have adopted an Aristotelian strategy to show that the most compelling purported counterexamples to grounding's status as a strict partial order are not genuine counterexamples after all, one might attempt to draw on different Aristotelian resources to admit their force while limiting the damage that they do to grounding's theoretical usefulness. Cameron (2014), aiming to defend the notion of grounding from the charge, made for various reasons by Koslicki (2015) and Wilson (2014), that it is equivocal, argues that we should understand 'ground' as an Aristotelian homonym, namely one for which there is a core sense and other (non-univocal) senses somehow depend upon it. This would, she says, allow variation in the formal properties of grounding. These properties could include, among others, asymmetry, irreflexivity, and transitivity. My proposal is not opposed to Cameron's overall suggestion about the benefits of understanding 'ground' as an Aristotelian homonym, though if I am right then it will not be any failure of asymmetry, irreflexivity, and transitivity that encourages us to think that 'ground' is non-univocal. I have not attempted to rule out other possible reasons for thinking that it is non-univocal and Cameron's suggestion might still be needed for addressing those, for all that I have said.

5.5 Grounding and Explanatory Relevance

Having said how Aristotle's solution to the Priority Problem would address the most compelling putative counterexamples to the claim that grounding induces a strict partial order, I want to end by saying something about why we should expect ontological priority or grounding to be qualification-sensitive when other comparative relations are not.[67] Ontological priority claims introduce qualification-sensitivity because they introduce a context of

---

[67] This issue grows out of an assertion by Bennett (2017, p. 44), mentioned previously (p. 42), that even if Lewisians had wanted to defend the irreflexivity of grounding by adverting to failures of intersubstitution, their counterpart-theoretic semantics would have afforded them

per se explanatory relevance.[68] For Aristotle, the *per se* explanatory relevance of x to y is revealed by correctly specifying x and y. Since, for Aristotle, every case of ontological priority has this qualification-sensitive structure, we know in advance that apparent counterexamples to the asymmetry, irreflexivity, and transitivity of ontological priority will be ubiquitous: Any case of ontological priority can seem problematic if we fail to observe the distinction between subjects and qualifications of them. Aristotle's account, then, not only responds to apparent counterexamples but also predicts and explains their ubiquity, thus addressing head-on a worry, expressed by Wilson (2014, p. 570) and endorsed by Bennett (2017, p. 38), that responding to apparent counterexamples is "increasingly ad hoc" as they become more numerous.

I find it plausible that grounding claims, like Aristotelian ontological priority claims, are qualification-sensitive because they introduce a context of *per se* explanatory relevance. (As I mentioned on p. 4 n. 9, there is broad, though not universal, support for thinking that grounding, like Aristotle's version of ontological priority, is explanatory, whether it is, involves, backs, or is accounted for by explanation.) If this is correct, then a principled response to ways of challenging grounding's order-theoretic properties is readily available: Grounding claims, being explanatory, do not license the *secundum quid ad simpliciter* or *simpliciter ad secundum quid* inferences on which the apparent counterexamples to grounding's asymmetry, irreflexivity, and transitivity depend. Note that this observation is compatible with, but distinct from, the claim (mentioned previously on p. 5) that grounding, like explanation, is hyperintensional. The latter claim tells us only that substitution even of necessary equivalents *can* fail in grounding contexts but not under what conditions it *does* fail or that it fails at least in the apparent counterexamples to grounding's asymmetry, irreflexivity, and transitivity.[69]

6 Conclusion

I have argued that Aristotle is committed to ontological priority being asymmetric, irreflexive, and transitive, and yet insists in numerous cases that one thing is ontologically prior to another even though it apparently fails to meet

---

no principled reason for supposing that grounding claims should trigger such failures when claims involving other comparative relations do not.

[68] There initially appear to be two exceptions for Aristotle, both of which I argued are merely apparent (p. 14).

[69] This point is an application of the observation that for hyperintensional notions in general, not only for grounding, the mere fact of hyperintensionality does not settle what kinds of substitution failures are to be expected for the notion in question. See Jespersen and Duží (2015, p. 527).

his conditions for ontological priority. I called this situation "the Priority Problem." That this apparent problem emerges from Aristotle's view is interesting on its own since current debates about whether metaphysical grounding has these features proceed as if Aristotle's theory of ontological priority, which some claim as origin of the notion of grounding, were silent on the matter. But furthermore, I have contended that Aristotle has a principled solution that both eliminates the threat from each of the apparently problematic examples and explains why such examples are ubiquitous. Finally, I have described how a ground-theoretic analog of Aristotle's solution to the Priority Problem would address the most compelling recent challenges to the claim that metaphysical grounding induces a strict partial order on its domain and have isolated the commitment that current theorists would require for adopting such a solution. This commitment is a reasonable price for a principled Aristotelian solution to an Aristotelian problem for an Aristotelian notion.

Appendix

Collected Descriptions

In the following definitions, '$\lhd$' expresses a relational predicate that features grounds to the left (with variable arity) and grounded to the right, '$\nlhd$' expresses the negation of this predicate, 'δ' expresses a relation that should be read as 'the difference between … on the one hand and … on the other,' ' … in contrast to … ,' ' … instead of … ,' or ' … rather than … ' The set X comprises obtaining facts, actually existing entities, and truths, whereas the set Y comprises non-obtaining facts, entities that do not actually exist, and falsehoods.

Correlatives "those things for which being is the same as being somehow related to something" (*Cat.* 7, 8^{a}31–32)

Distinctions

Conceptual distinction Introduced entirely by our way of cognizing or describing, e.g., Polycleitus vs. Polycleitus cognized/described as sculpting

***Realis major* distinction** Worldly numerical distinctness, e.g., Polycleitus vs. the mereological sum of Polycleitus and sculpting

***Realis minor* distinction** Intermediate between conceptual and *realis major* distinctions: compatible with numerical sameness but featuring a distinction with a worldly basis, such as one in form, mode, *vel sim.*, e.g., Polycleitus vs. a mode/formality of Polycleitus

Pluralism The distinction between a subject and a qualification of that subject can be construed in more than one of these ways depending on the case at issue.

Expansion

Expansion intolerance

$$\forall x, y, z\big(x \lhd y \rightarrow (z \nlhd y \rightarrow x \wedge z \nlhd y)\big)$$

Informally: Any true grounding claim is falsified by adding to the ground an item that does not ground the grounded.

Proliferation intolerance There are no distinct grounds of the same grounded where the distinction results from the introduction of items that do not ground the grounded. In other words, non-grounds never make the grounded ground-theoretically overdetermined.

Wide differential expansion intolerance

$$\forall xy \in X, \forall x^*y^*z \in Y\big(\delta xx^* \lhd \delta yy^* \rightarrow \big((\delta xz \nlhd \delta yy^*) \rightarrow (\delta xx^* \wedge \delta xz \nlhd \delta yy^*)\big)\big)$$

Informally: The conjunction of any difference that grounds a second difference with any difference that does not ground the second difference also does not ground the second difference.

Narrow differential expansion intolerance

$$\forall xy \in X, \forall x^*y^*z \in Y\left(\delta xx^* \lhd \delta yy^* \rightarrow \left((\delta xz \ntriangleleft \delta yy^*) \rightarrow (\delta xx^*z \ntriangleleft \delta yy^*)\right)\right)$$

Informally: Any difference that grounds a second difference fails to ground it when its terms are supplemented by a non-obtaining term of a difference that does not ground the second difference.

Non-monotonicity

Weak non-monotonicity $\neg\forall x, y, z(x \lhd y \rightarrow x \wedge z \lhd y)$

Strong non-monotonicity $\forall x, y, z(x \lhd y \rightarrow x \wedge z \ntriangleleft y)$

Order-Theoretic Properties of Grounding

	Predicate	*Sentential operator*
asymmetric	$\forall x, y(x \lhd y \rightarrow y \ntriangleleft x)$	$\dfrac{\phi < \psi \qquad \psi < \phi}{\bot}$
irreflexive	$\forall x(x \ntriangleleft x)$	$\dfrac{\phi < \phi}{\bot}$
transitive	$\forall x, y, z(x \lhd y \wedge y \lhd z \rightarrow x \lhd z)$	$\dfrac{\phi < \psi \qquad \psi < \theta}{\phi < \theta}$

Kinds of Priority in Categories 12

Temporal priority Priority in time (e.g., older is prior to younger)

Implicative priority Priority in nonreciprocal implication of being (e.g., two implies the being of one but not vice versa)

Positional priority Priority in arrangement (e.g., elements are prior to diagrams, the proëm is prior to the main narrative)

Axiological priority Priority in value (e.g., someone loved more has priority over someone loved less)

Explanatory priority Priority in causation/explanation where implication of being is reciprocal (e.g., Man/a man/a man's being/that there is a man is prior to a true *logos* concerning him/it)

Kinds of Priority in Metaphysics 5.11

Positional priority Nearer some starting point that is specified absolutely and by nature or relatively

1. Place (closer to the specified spatial starting point)
2. Time (further from now for past events, closer to now for future events)

3. Change (closer to the starting point of change)
4. Capacity (more capable of initiating change)
5. Arrangement (e.g., the person second to the leader of a chorus is prior to the person third from the leader)

Cognitive priority Prior in cognition

1. Account (what is clearer and more intelligible in its own right, e.g., the universal is prior to the particular)
2. Perception (what is clearer and more intelligible from the point of view of our perception, e.g., the particular is prior to the universal)

Derivative priority Prior as a property of what is prior (e.g., straightness of lines is prior to smoothness of surfaces since lines are prior to surfaces)
Ontological priority Prior in nature and substance

1. Categorial (substance, as subject, is prior to…)
2. Potentiality (e.g., matter is prior to substance, part is prior to whole)
3. Actuality (e.g., substance is prior to matter, whole is prior to part)

Priority

Existential priority For all x and all y, x is existentially ontologically prior to y if and only if x can exist without y existing but y cannot exist without x existing.
Essential priority For all x and all y, x is essentially ontologically prior to y if and only if x can be what x is without y being what y is but y cannot be what y is without x being what x is.
Ontic priority For all x and all y, x is ontically prior to y if and only if x has the ontological status of a being independently of standing in some tie to y, but y has its ontological status in virtue of (that is to say, grounded in) standing in a tie to x.
Priority Problem If Aristotle thinks that there are cases in which, for some x and some y, x is prior to y and x and y are correlatives, then it would be true both that x can be without y (because of the priority of x to y) and that x cannot be without y (because of their correlativity), which would be a contradiction. He appears to think that there are such cases.

References

Ackrill, J. (1963). *Aristotle:* Categories *and* De Interpretatione. Clarendon Press.

Ackrill, J. (1981). *Aristotle the philosopher*. Clarendon Press.

Ainsworth, T. (2018). Priority in being in Aristotle. *Philosophy Compass, 13*. https://doi.org/10.1111/phc3.12483.

Alexander of Aphrodisias. (1883). *In Aristotelis analyticorum priorum librum i commentarium* (M. Wallies, Ed.; Vol. 2.1). Reimer.

Alexander of Aphrodisias. (1891). *In Aristotelis topicorum libros octo commentaria* (M. Wallies, Ed.; Vol. 2.2). Reimer.

Ammonius. (1895). *In Aristotelis categorias commentarius* (A. Busse, Ed.; Vol. 4.4). Reimer.

Anonymous. (1883). *Categoriarum paraphrasis* (M. Hayduck, Ed.; Vol. 23.2). Reimer.

Audi, P. (2012). Grounding: Towards a theory of the in-virtue-of relation. *The Journal of Philosophy, 109*, 685–711.

Audi, P. (2020). Why truthmaking is not a case of grounding. *Philosophy and Phenomenological Research, 101*, 567–590.

Averroes. (1983). *Averroes' middle commentaries on Aristotle's* Categories *and* De interpretatione (C. E. Butterworth, Trans.). Princeton University Press.

Bäck, A. T. (1996). *On reduplication: Logical theories of qualification*. Brill.

Barnes, E. (2018). Symmetric dependence. In R. Bliss & G. Priest (Eds.), *Reality and its structure: Essays in fundamentality* (pp. 50–69). Oxford University Press.

Baxter, D. L. M. (2018). Self-differing, aspects, and Leibniz's law. *Noûs, 52*, 900–920.

Beere, J. (2009). *Doing and being: An interpretation of Aristotle's* Metaphysics Theta. Oxford University Press.

Bennett, K. (2017). *Making things up*. Oxford University Press.

Berker, S. (2018). The unity of grounding. *Mind, 127*, 729–777.

Blander, J. (2020). Same as it never was: John Duns Scotus' Paris *Reportatio* account of identity and distinction. *British Journal for the History of Philosophy, 28*, 231–250.

Bliss, R. (2014). Viciousness and circles of ground. *Metaphilosophy, 45*, 245–256.

Bliss, R. (2018). Grounding and reflexivity. In R. Bliss & G. Priest (Eds.), *Reality and its structure: Essays in fundamentality* (pp. 70–90). Oxford University Press.

Bodéüs, R. (2001). *Aristote: Catégories*. Les Belles Lettres.

Bolzano, B. (1837). *Wissenschaftslehre: Versuch einer ausführlichen und grösstentheils neuen Darstellung der Logik mit steter Rücksicht auf deren bisherige Bearbeiter* (Vol. 2). J. E. v. Seidel.

Cameron, M. (2014). Is ground said-in-many-ways? *Studia Philosophica Estonica, 7*, 29–55.

Cameron, M. (2020). Medieval and early modern. In M. J. Raven (Ed.), *The Routledge handbook of metaphysical grounding* (pp. 49–62). Routledge.

Charles, D. (1984). *Aristotle's philosophy of action*. Duckworth.

Charles, D. (2021). *The undivided self: Aristotle and the 'mind-body problem'*. Oxford University Press.

Cleary, J. J. (1988). *Aristotle on the many senses of priority*. Southern Illinois University Press.

Cohen, S. M. (2008). Kooky objects revisited: Aristotle's ontology. *Metaphilosophy, 39*, 3–19.

Corkum, P. (2008). Aristotle on ontological dependence. *Phronesis, 53*, 65–92.

Corkum, P. (2013a). Critical notice for Michail Peramatzis's *Priority in Aristotle's Metaphysics*. *Canadian Journal of Philosophy, 43*, 136–156.

Corkum, P. (2013b). Substance and independence in Aristotle. In M. Hoeltje, B. Schnieder, & A. Steinberg (Eds.), *Varieties of dependence: Ontological dependence, grounding, supervenience, response-dependence* (pp. 65–95). Philosophia Verlag.

Corkum, P. (2016). Ontological dependence and grounding in Aristotle. *Oxford Handbooks Online in Philosophy*. https://doi.org/10.1093/oxfordhb/9780199935314.013.31.

Corkum, P. (2020). Ancient. In M. J. Raven (Ed.), *The Routledge handbook of metaphysical grounding* (pp. 20–31). Routledge.

Correia, F. (2005). *Existential dependence and cognate notions*. Philosophia Verlag.

Correia, F. (2010). Grounding and truth-functions. *Logique et Analyse, 53*, 251–279.

Correia, F. (2024). *The logic of grounding*. Cambridge University Press.

Crivelli, P. (2004). *Aristotle on truth*. Cambridge University Press.

Dancy, R. M. (1975). On some of Aristotle's first thoughts about substances. *The Philosophical Review, 87*, 372–413.

Dancy, R. M. (1981). Aristotle and the priority of actuality. In S. Knuuttila (Ed.), *Reforging the great chain of being: Studies in the history of modal theories* (pp. 73–115). Springer.

Dasgupta, S. (2014). On the plurality of grounds. *Philosophers' Imprint, 14,* 1–28.

Dasgupta, S. (2017). Constitutive explanation. *Philosophical Issues, 27,* 74–97.

De Morgan, A. (1856). On the symbols of logic, the theory of the syllogism, and in particular of the copula, and the application of the theory of probabilities to some questions of evidence. *Transactions of the Cambridge Philosophical Society, 9,* 79–127.

deRosett, L. (2013). Grounding explanations. *Philosophers' Imprint, 13,* 1–26.

deRosett, L. (2023). *Fundamental things: Theory and applications of grounding.* Oxford University Press.

Duncombe, M. (2015). Aristotle's two accounts of relatives in *Categories* 7. *Phronesis, 60,* 436–461.

Duncombe, M. (2020). *Ancient relativity: Plato, Aristotle, Stoics, and Sceptics.* Oxford University Press.

Edelhoff, A. L. (2020). *Aristotle on ontological priority in the* Categories. Cambridge University Press.

Elias. (1900). *In Porphyrii isagogen et Aristotelis categorias commentaria* (A. Busse, Ed.; Vol. 18.1). Reimer.

Embry, B. (2018). Sebastián Izquierdo's (1601–1681) theory of priority. *Journal of the American Philosophical Association, 4,* 491–509.

al-Fārābī. (1957). Paraphrase of the *Categories* of Aristotle (D. M. Dunlop, Ed. & Trans.). *The Islamic Quarterly, 4,* 168–183.

Fine, G. (1984). Separation. *Oxford Studies in Ancient Philosophy, 2,* 31–87.

Fine, K. (1982). Acts, events and things. In W. Leinfellner & E. Kraemer (Eds.), *Language and ontology: Proceedings of the 6th international Wittgenstein symposium* (pp. 97–105). Holder-Pichler-Tempsky.

Fine, K. (1995). Ontological dependence. *Proceedings of the Aristotelian Society, 95,* 269–290.

Fine, K. (2001). The question of realism. *Philosophers' Imprint, 1,* 1–30.

Fine, K. (2010). Some puzzles of ground. *Notre Dame Journal of Formal Logic, 51,* 97–118.

Fine, K. (2012). Guide to ground. In F. Correia & B. Schnieder (Eds.), *Metaphysical grounding: Understanding the structure of reality* (pp. 37–80). Cambridge University Press.

Glazier, M. (2020). Explanation. In M. J. Raven (Ed.), *The Routledge handbook of metaphysical grounding* (pp. 121–131). Routledge.

Goodman, J. (2023). Grounding generalizations. *Journal of Philosophical Logic, 52*, 821–858.

Gottlieb, P. (1993). Aristotle versus Protagoras on relatives and the objects of perception. *Oxford Studies in Ancient Philosophy, 11*, 101–119.

Graham, D. (1999). *Aristotle:* Physics *book viii*. Oxford University Press.

Guigon, G. (2018). Truths *qua* grounds. *Philosophy and Phenomenological Research, 97*, 99–125.

Harari, O. (2011). The unity of Aristotle's category of relatives. *Classical Quarterly, 61*, 521–537.

Hennig, B. (2024). Qualification in philosophy. *Acta Analytica, 39*, 183–205.

Hood, P. M. (2004). *Aristotle on the category of relation*. University Press of America.

Izquierdo, S. (1659). *Pharus scientiarum* (Vol. 2). Bourgeat; Liétard.

Jenkins, C. (2011). Is metaphysical dependence irreflexive? *The Monist, 94*, 267–276.

Jespersen, B., & Duží, M. (2015). Introduction. *Synthese, 192*, 525–534.

John Duns Scotus. (1891). *Reportata Parisiensa liber primus, dist. i-xlviii et liber secundus, dist. i-xi* (L. Wadding, Ed.; Vol. 22). Vivès.

John Duns Scotus. (2009). *Abhandlung über das erste Prinzip (Tractatus de primo principio)* (W. Kluxen, Ed. & Trans.; 4th ed.). Wissenschaftliche Buchgesellschaft.

John Duns Scotus. (2024). *Treatise on the first principle* (T. M. Ward, Trans.). Hackett.

John of Damascus. (1969). *Die Schriften des Johannes von Damaskos* (B. Kotter, Ed.; Vol. 1). De Gruyter.

Katz, E. (2017). Ontological separation in Aristotle's metaphysics. *Phronesis, 62*, 26–68.

Kelsey, S. (2022). *Mind and world in Aristotle's* De Anima. Cambridge University Press.

Kirwan, C. (1971). *Aristotle:* Metaphysics *books* Γ, Δ, *and* E. Clarendon Press.

Korbmacher, J. (2018a). Axiomatic theories of partial ground i: The base theory. *Journal of Philosophical Logic, 47*, 161–191.

Korbmacher, J. (2018b). Axiomatic theories of partial ground ii: Partial ground and hierarchies of typed truth. *Journal of Philosophical Logic, 47*, 193–226.

Koslicki, K. (2015). The coarse-grainedness of grounding. *Oxford Studies in Metaphysics, 9*, 306–344.

Koslicki, K. (2018). *Form, matter, substance*. Oxford University Press.

Koslicki, K. (2020). Skeptical doubts. In M. J. Raven (Ed.), *The Routledge handbook of metaphysical grounding* (pp. 164–179). Routledge.

Kovacs, D. M. (2022). An explanatory idealist theory of grounding. *Noûs, 56,* 530–553.

Lear, J. (1982). Aristotle's philosophy of mathematics. *The Philosophical Review, 91,* 161–192.

Lederman, H. (2014). *Ho pote on esti* and coupled entities: A form of explanation in Aristotle's natural philosophy. *Oxford Studies in Ancient Philosophy, 46,* 109–164.

Lewis, D. K. (2003). Things qua truthmakers. In H. Lillehammer & G. Rodriguez-Pereyra (Eds.), *Real metaphysics: Essays in honour of D. H. Mellor* (pp. 25–38). Routledge.

Lewis, F. A. (1982). Accidental sameness in Aristotle. *Philosophical Studies, 42,* 1–36.

Litland, J. E. (2013). On some counterexamples to the transitivity of grounding. *Essays in Philosophy, 14.* https://doi.org/10.7710/1526-0569.1453.

Litland, J. E. (2015). Grounding, explanation, and the limit of internality. *The Philosophical Review, 124,* 481–532.

Loets, A. J. (2021). *Qua* qualification. *Philosophers' Imprint, 21*(27), 1–24.

Makin, S. (2003). What does Aristotle mean by priority in substance? *Oxford Studies in Ancient Philosophy, 24,* 209–238.

Malink, M. (2013). Essence and being: A discussion of Michail Peramatzis, *Priority in Aristotle's Metaphysics. Oxford Studies in Ancient Philosophy, 45,* 341–362.

Malink, M. (2020). Aristotelian demonstration. In M. J. Raven (Ed.), *The Routledge handbook of metaphysical grounding* (pp. 33–48). Routledge.

Malink, M. (2022). Aristotle and Bolzano on grounding. In S. Roski & B. Schnieder (Eds.), *Bolzano's philosophy of grounding: Translations and studies* (pp. 221–243). Oxford University Press.

Matthews, G. (1982). Accidental unities. In M. Schofield & M. Nussbaum (Eds.), *Language and logos* (pp. 223–240). Cambridge University Press.

Maurin, A.-S. (2019). Grounding and metaphysical explanation: It's complicated. *Philosophical Studies, 176,* 1573–1594.

Meadows, K. (2023). Causal priority in *Metaphysics* θ.8. *Archiv für Geschichte der Philosophie, 105,* 197–240.

Meister, S. (2020). Aristotle on the purity of forms in *Metaphysics* Z.10–11. *Ergo: An Open Access Journal of Philosophy, 7.* https://doi.org/10.3998/ergo .12405314.0007.001

Merlo, G. (2022). Disjunction and the logic of grounding. *Erkenntnis, 87,* 567–587.

Mesquita, A. P. (2025). *Aristotle on natural simultaneity of relatives in the* Categories. Routledge.

Mignucci, M. (1986). Aristotle's definitions of relatives in *Cat. 7*. *Phronesis, 31*, 101–127.

Miller, F. D. (1973). Did Aristotle have the concept of identity? *The Philosophical Review, 82*, 483–490.

Morales, F. (1994). Relational attributes in Aristotle. *Phronesis, 39*, 255–274.

Moravcsik, J. (1975). *Aitia* as generative factor in Aristotle's philosophy. *Dialogue, 14*, 622–638.

Nolan, D. (2018). Cosmic loops. In R. Bliss & G. Priest (Eds.), *Reality and its structure: Essays in fundamentality* (pp. 91–106). Oxford University Press.

Nolan, D. (2026). Grounding, explanation, and the task of metaphysics. In A. Segal & N. Stang (Eds.), *Systematic metaphysics: Historical and contemporary perspectives*. Oxford University Press.

Oehler, K. (2006). *Aristoteles Kategorien*. Akademie Verlag.

Olympiodorus. (1902). *Prolegomena et in categorias commentarium* (A. Busse, Ed.; Vol. 12.1). Reimer.

Panayides, C. Y. (1999). Aristotle on the priority of actuality in substance. *Ancient Philosophy, 19*, 327–344.

Peramatzis, M. (2008). Aristotle's notion of priority in nature and substance. *Oxford Studies in Ancient Philosophy, 35*, 187–247.

Peramatzis, M. (2011). *Priority in Aristotle's metaphysics*. Oxford University Press.

Philoponus. (1898). *In Aristotelis categorias commentarium* (A. Busse, Ed.; Vol. 13.1). Reimer.

Primavesi, O. (Ed.). (2018). *Aristoteles über die Bewegung der Lebewesen*, De motu animalium (K. Corcilius, Trans.). Meiner.

Raven, M. J. (2013). Is ground a strict partial order? *American Philosophical Quarterly, 50*, 191–199.

Reece, B. C. (2019). Aristotle's four causes of action. *Australasian Journal of Philosophy, 97*, 213–227.

Reece, B. C. (2023). *Aristotle on happiness, virtue, and wisdom*. Cambridge University Press.

Reece, B. C. (2024). Theophrastus on intellect in Aristotle's *De Anima*. *Proceedings of the Boston Area Colloquium in Ancient Philosophy, 38*, 1–27.

Reece, B. C. (ms-a). Grounding and the work of philosophy. In R. Neels (Ed.), *Ground and fundamentality in Plato and Aristotle*. Routledge.

Reece, B. C. (ms-b). How to make any science a science of everything.

Reeve, C. (2016). *Aristotle:* Metaphysics (C. Reeve, Trans.). Hackett.

Rodriguez-Pereyra, G. (2015). Grounding is not a strict order. *Journal of the American Philosophical Association, 1*, 517–534.

Rosen, G. (2010). Metaphysical dependence: Grounding and reduction. In B. Hale & A. Hoffman (Eds.), *Modality: Metaphysics, logic, and epistemology* (pp. 109–136). Oxford University Press.

Roski, S. (2020). Bolzano. In M. J. Raven (Ed.), *The Routledge handbook of metaphysical grounding* (pp. 76–89). Routledge.

Roski, S., & Schnieder, B. (Eds.). (2022). *Bolzano's philosophy of grounding: Translations and studies*. Oxford University Press.

Ross, W. (1924). *Aristotle's* Metaphysics: *A revised text with introduction and commentary*. Clarendon Press.

Rubenstein, E. (2024). Two approaches to metaphysical explanation. *Noûs, 58*, 1107–1136.

Schaffer, J. (2009). On what grounds what. In D. Manley & D. Chalmers (Eds.), *Metametaphysics: New essays on the foundations of ontology* (pp. 347–383). Oxford University Press.

Schaffer, J. (2012). Grounding, transitivity, and contrastivity. In F. Correia & B. Schnieder (Eds.), *Metaphysical grounding: Understanding the structure of reality* (pp. 122–138). Cambridge University Press.

Schaffer, J. (2016). Grounding in the image of causation. *Philosophical Studies, 173*, 49–100.

Schnieder, B. (2011). A logic for 'because'. *Review of Symbolic Logic, 4*, 445–465.

Schnieder, B. (2014). Bolzano on causation and grounding. *Journal of the History of Philosophy, 52*, 309–337.

Schnieder, B. (2020). Grounding and dependence. *Synthese, 197*, 95–124.

Schnieder, B., & Werner, J. (2021). An Aristotelian approach to existential dependence. In L. Jansen & P. Sandstad (Eds.), *Neo-Aristotelian perspectives on formal causation* (pp. 151–174). Routledge.

Sedley, D. (2002). Aristotelian relativities. In M. Canto-Sperber & P. Pellegrin (Eds.), *Le style de la pensée: Recueil de textes en hommage à Jacques Brunschwig* (pp. 324–352). Les Belles Lettres.

Sergius of Rešᶜainā. (2016). *Introduction to Aristotle and his* Categories, *addressed to Philotheos* (S. Aydin, Ed. & Trans.). Brill.

Sergius of Rešᶜainā. (2024). *Commentary on Aristotle's* Categories (Y. Arzhanov, Ed. & Trans.). De Gruyter.

Simplicius. (1907). *In Aristotelis categorias commentarium* (K. Kalbfleisch, Ed.; Vol. 8). Reimer.

Sirkel, R. (2024). Ontological priority and grounding in Aristotle's *Categories*. In C. G. Normore & S. Schmid (Eds.), *Grounding in medieval philosophy* (pp. 33–63). Springer.

Siscoe, R. W. (2022). Grounding, understanding, and explanation. *Pacific Philosophical Quarterly, 103*, 791–815.

Skiles, A., & Trogdon, K. (2021). Should explanation be a guide to ground? *Philosophical Studies, 178*, 4083–4098.

Sorabji, R. (1980). *Necessity, cause, and blame: Perspectives on Aristotle's theory*. Cornell University Press.

Spellman, L. (1995). *Substance and separation in Aristotle*. Cambridge University Press.

Stein, N. (2012). Causal necessity in Aristotle. *British Journal for the History of Philosophy, 20*, 855–879.

Suárez, F. (1861). *Disputationes metaphysicae 1-27* (C. Berton, Ed.; Vol. 25). Vivès.

Szabó, Z. G. (2003). On qualification. *Philosophical Perspectives, 17*, 385–414.

Tahko, T. (2013). Truth-grounding and transitivity. *Thought, 2*, 332–340.

Thompson, N. (2016a). Grounding and metaphysical explanation. *Proceedings of the Aristotelian Society, 116*, 395–402.

Thompson, N. (2016b). Metaphysical interdependence. In M. Jago (Ed.), *Reality making* (pp. 39–56). Oxford University Press.

Thompson, N. (2018). Metaphysical interdependence, epistemic coherentism, and holistic explanation. In R. Bliss & G. Priest (Eds.), *Reality and its structure: Essays in fundamentality* (pp. 107–125). Oxford University Press.

Thompson, N. (2020). Strict partial order. In M. J. Raven (Ed.), *The Routledge handbook of metaphysical grounding* (pp. 259–270). Routledge.

Trogdon, K. (2013). An introduction to grounding. In M. Hoeltje & B. Schnieder (Eds.), *Varieties of dependence: Ontological dependence, grounding, supervenience, response-dependence* (pp. 97–122). Philosophia Verlag.

Wang, J. (2020). Cause. In M. J. Raven (Ed.), *The Routledge handbook of metaphysical grounding* (pp. 300–310). Routledge.

Wilhelm, I. (2020). An argument for entity grounding. *Analysis, 80*, 500–507.

Wilhelm, I. (2021). Grounding and propositional identity. *Analysis, 81*, 80–81.

Williams, C. (1985). Aristotle's theory of descriptions. *The Philosophical Review, 94*, 63–80.

Wilson, A. (2018). Metaphysical causation. *Noûs, 52*, 723–751.

Wilson, J. (2014). No work for a theory of grounding. *Inquiry, 57*, 1–45.

Witt, C. (1994). The priority of actuality. In T. Scaltsas, D. Charles, & M. L. Gill (Eds.), *Unity, identity, and explanation in Aristotle's metaphysics* (pp. 215–228). Oxford University Press.

Yablo, S. (1987). Identity, essence, and indiscernibility. *The Journal of Philosophy, 84*, 293–314.

Zanatta, M. (1989). *Aristotele: Le categorie*. Biblioteca Universale Rizzoli.

Acknowledgments

I wish to thank Peter Adamson, Yury Arzhanov, Donald Baxter, Jeffrey Brower, Eric Brown, Margaret Cameron, David Charles, James Van Cleve, Phil Corkum, Matthew Duncombe, Brian Embry, Robert Garcia, Yoaav Isaacs, Dhananjay Jagannathan, Rusty Jones, Emily Katz, Harvey Lederman, William Lycan, Katy Meadows, Marko Malink, Michail Peramatzis, Alexander Pruss, Michael Raven, Jonathan Schaffer, Christopher Shields, Riin Sirkel, Rohan Sud, Thomas Ward, James Warren, Isaac Wilhelm, Dean Zimmerman, and anonymous referees for helpful conversations and feedback. Michail Peramatzis, in particular, was helpful at various stages of this work. James Warren made valuable editorial suggestions. Parts were presented at the 2019 American Philosophical Association Eastern Divisional Meeting, Toronto Metropolitan University, and the University of Connecticut. I am grateful to the members of the audience on each occasion for helpful feedback.

Work on this project was generously supported through two fellowships: a Fellowship in Hellenic Studies at Harvard University's Center for Hellenic Studies (CHS) in 2018–2019, and the John and Daria Barry Postdoctoral Fellowship at the University of Chicago's Department of Philosophy in 2019–2020. Among those at the CHS I want in particular to thank Gregory Nagy, Mark Schiefsky, Zoie Lafis, and Richard Martin. I am grateful, too, for the kind assistance of the CHS library staff: Erika Bainbridge, Lanah Koelle, Sophie Boisseau, Michael Strickland, and Temple Wright. From the University of Chicago I would especially like to thank Candace Vogler and Michael Kremer, as well as the John and Daria Barry Foundation for making the fellowship possible.

My research has frequently been aided by the *Diogenes* open-source software application developed by P. J. Heslin, as well as by the Perseus Digital Library.

Finally, I wish to thank my wife and children for their patience with this endeavor.

Ancient Philosophy

James Warren
University of Cambridge

James Warren is Professor of Ancient Philosophy at the University of Cambridge. He is the author of *Epicurus and Democritean Ethics* (Cambridge, 2002), *Facing Death: Epicurus and his Critics* (2004), *Presocratics* (2007) and *The Pleasures of Reason in Plato, Aristotle and the Hellenistic Hedonists* (Cambridge, 2014). He is also the editor of *The Cambridge Companion to Epicurus* (Cambridge, 2009), and joint editor of *Authors and Authorities in Ancient Philosophy* (Cambridge, 2018).

About the Series

The Elements in Ancient Philosophy series deals with a wide variety of topics and texts in ancient Greek and Roman philosophy, written by leading scholars in the field. Taking a theme, question, or type of argument, some Elements explore it across antiquity and beyond. Others look in detail at an ancient author, a specific work, or a part of a longer work, considering its structure, content, and significance, or explore more directly ancient perspectives on modern philosophical questions.

For EU product safety concerns, contact us at Calle de José Abascal, 56–1°, 28003 Madrid, Spain or eugpsr@cambridge.org.